BLOOM
Founded by | arihant

Olympiad ACE

A Comprehensive Practice Book

for School Olympiads & Talent Search Exams

GENERAL KNOWLEDGE

Class 8

by

Suman Bharti

Olympiad ACE

BLOOM

Bloom Cap Edu Ventures Pvt. Ltd.

卐 **Administrative & Production Office**

'Ramchhaya' 4577/15, Agarwal Road, Darya Ganj, New Delhi -110002
Tele: 011- 47630600, 43518550

卐 **PRICE:** ₹125.00

Published by Arihant Publications (I) Ltd.

For further information about the books log on to
www.bloomcap.org

Follow us on

Preface

"Future belongs to those Who prepares for it today"

School Olympiads are National & International level competitions conducted by different Government, Non-Government & Educational Organisations with the purpose of making the children ready to face competitive exams. The challenging Questions asked in Olympiads motivate them to learn more & more and bring out the best result with improved academic performance. The Awards & Scholarship offered by Olympiads motivate children to aspire & strive for doing better and emerge out to be the best.

GK Olympiads

GK is the knowledge of every aspect of the human life, which may or may not be the part of routine academic studies but very important for the overall personality development of the students. It is more or less connected with the attentiveness and awareness. There can be different domains of GK like; History, Geography, Polity, Culture, Discovery, Sports, Current Affairs etc.

GK Olympiads help students in understanding the importance of General Knowledge and updations about National & International Affairs in daily life.

'Bloom GK Olympiad Study Book Class 8' is a perfect resource to Study & Practice for Olympiad Exams and other National & State Level Talent Search Exams & Other Competitions.

Some Special Features of Bloom GK Olympiad Study Books are;

- Complete coverage of all the topics related to GK;. History, Geography, Environment, Polity, Science, Sports, etc.
- Chapterwise Exercises having different types of Objective Questions.
- Olympiad Pattern Practice Sets at the end.

This book is prepared by Expert Panel with the utmost care, still if you have any suggestions regarding its improvement then feel free to contact us at support@bloomcap.org. We will try to inculcate your suggestions in the further editions.

Contents

Chapter 01

History of India and the World

MCQs 1 Mark Questions

1. Who among the following was the author of Buddhacharita?
(a) Kautilya (b) Ashvaghosa
(c) Kalidasa (d) Nagasena

2. King Ashoka belonged to which of the following dynasties?
(a) Haryanka (b) Gupta
(c) Maurya (d) Sungas

3. The terms Dhamma and Stupas are related to which of the following religions?
(a) Jainism
(b) Hinduism
(c) Parsi
(d) Buddhism

4. Razia Sultan and Jalal-ud-din Khalji were the rulers of ....
(a) Golconda (b) Delhi
(c) Awadh (d) Kanpur

5. The term Jizya was related to measure the unit of which of the following?
(a) Crop (b) Water
(c) Tax (d) Cattle

6. The ruler of Delhi Sultanate Iltutmish was the ruler of ....
(a) Slave Dynasty (b) Khalji Dynasty
(c) Tughlaq Dynasty (d) Lodi Dynasty

7. Select the correct chronology of the rulers of Delhi Sultanate.
(a) Iltutmish, Alauddin Khalji, Firoz Shah Tughlaq, Ibrahim Lodi
(b) Ibrahim Lodi, Iltutmish, Firoz Shah Tughlaq, Alauddin Khalji
(c) Alauddin Khalji, Ibrahim Lodi, Firoz Shah Tughlaq, Iltutmish,
(d) Firoz Shah Tughlaq ,Alauddin Khalji, Iltutmish, Ibrahim Lodi

8. The Second Battle of Panipat was fought between which among the following?
(a) Hemu and Akbar
(b) Marathas and Afghans
(c) Babar and Ibrahim Lodi
(d) Akbar and Marathas

9. Who among the following introduced the idea of Sulh-i-kul?
(a) Firoz Shah Tughlaq
(b) Akbar
(c) Jahangir
(d) Sher Shah Suri

10. Mansabdari system was related to which of the following?
(a) Cropping (b) Administrative
(c) Revenue (d) Irrigation

11. Identify the correctly matched pair.

	Rulers		Empire/Dynasty
(a)	Qutb-ud-Din Aibak	–	Slave Dynasty
(b)	Krishnadeva Raya	–	Pala Kingdom
(c)	Humayun	–	Vijayanagara Empire
(d)	Ibrahim Lodi	–	Sayyid Dynasty

12. The city of Siri in Delhi was founded by ....
(a) Alauddin Khalji
(b) Iltutmish
(c) Akbar
(d) Shah Jahan

13. Who was known as 'Rangrez' among the following professions?
(a) Farmers (b) Dyer
(c) Merchants (d) Traders

14. Who among the following were the first Europeans to land on Indian sub-continent?
(a) French (b) Portuguese
(c) Britishers (d) Dutch

15. Who among the following was the first Governor-General of Bengal?
(a) Warren Hastings
(b) Lord Cornwallis
(c) Lord Wellesley
(d) Lord Minto

16. Complete the given analogy.
Rani Lakshmi Bai : Jhansi :: Veer Kunwar Singh : ?
(a) Kanpur (b) Awadh
(c) Bihar (d) Delhi

17. The Sati Pratha was related to which of the following practices?
(a) Widow sacrifice
(b) Widow remarriage
(c) Child marriage
(d) Untouchability

18. .... was also known as the 'Father of Indian Reform'.
(a) BR Ambedkar
(b) Dayananda Saraswati
(c) Ishwar Chandra Vidyasagar
(d) Raja Ram Mohan Roy

19. Which among the following personalities was related to Widow Remarriage Act?
(a) Ishwar Chandra Vidyasagar
(b) Dayananda Saraswati
(c) Ramakrishna Paramhans
(d) Raja Ram Mohan Roy

20. .... is also known as the first female teacher and social reformer.
(a) Mother Teresa
(b) Sarojini Naidu
(c) Savitribai Phule
(d) Vijaya Lakshmi Pandit

21. The Wood's Dispatch was related to which among the following?
(a) Education (b) Land Reform
(c) Military (d) Revenue

22. Identify the incorrectly matched pair.

	Personality		Institution founded
(a)	Swami Dayananda Saraswati	–	Prarthana Samaj
(b)	Raja Ram Mohan Roy	–	Brahmo Samaj
(c)	Swami Vivekananda	–	Ramakrishna Mission
(d)	Sayyid Ahmad Khan	–	Aligarh Muslim Unity

23. Anandamath, a Bengali historical novel was written by ....
(a) Rabindranath Tagore
(b) Bankim Chandra Chatterjee
(c) Premchand
(d) Dayananda Saraswati

24. Which among the following was not an extremist leader?
(a) Lala Lajpat Rai
(b) Dadabhai Naoroji
(c) Bal Gangadhar Tilak
(d) Bipin Chandra Pal

25. Who said "Swaraj is my birth-right and I shall have it"?
(a) Mahatma Gandhi
(b) Jawaharlal Nehru
(c) Vinoba Bhave
(d) Bal Gangadhar Tilak

26. When did the establishment of Indian National Congress take place?
(a) 1886
(b) 1885
(c) 1887
(d) 1888

27. The first session of Indian National Congress was presided by............ .
(a) Womesh Chandra Bonnerjee
(b) Dadabhai Naoroji
(c) Badruddin Tyabji
(d) Pherozeshah Mehta

28. Which of the group of powers were collectively known as the axis power during the World War II?
(a) France, Japan, Italy
(b) Japan, Germany, Turkey
(c) Austria, Germany, Italy
(d) Germany, Italy, Japan

29. The USSR finally collapsed in which of the following years?
(a) 1985 (b) 1889 (c) 1991 (d) 1993

30. Who was the President of USA during World War I?
(a) Winston Churchill
(b) Joseph Stalin
(c) Franklin D Roosevelt
(d) Harry S Truman

31. Which of the following treaties led to the end of World War I?
(a) Treaty of Versailles
(b) Treaty of Brussels
(c) Treaty of Paris
(d) Treaty of Westphalia

32. The ideas of liberty, equality and fraternity were popularised during which revolution in the world history?
(a) Chinese Revolution
(b) French Revolution
(c) American Revolution
(d) Glorious Revolution

33. Which country bombed the cities of Hiroshima and Nagasaki during World War II?
(a) USA (b) France (c) Italy (d) UK

34. Which event led to the end of Cold War?
(a) Disintegration of USSR
(b) Freedom of Russia
(c) Freedom of America
(d) Fall of Berlin Wall

35. .... is also known as the 'Grand Old Man of India'.
(a) Dadabhai Naoroji
(b) Womesh Chandra Bonnerjee
(c) Pherozeshah Mehta
(d) Badruddin Tyabji

36. Read the following statements and select the correct option.

(a) Mahatma Gandhi was an extremist leader.

(b) The Doctrine of Lapse was introduced by Warren Hastings.

(c) Annie Besant was the first woman President of Indian National Congress .

(d) Rabindranath Tagore wrote the national song of India.

MCQs 2 Marks Questions

37. Read the following statements and select the correct option.

I. Kautilya belonged to the royal court of Bimbisara.

II. Harihara and Bukka founded the Vijayanagara Empire.

III. Hiuen Tsang was a Mongolian Traveller.

IV. King Harshvardhana was the ruler of Pushyabhuti Dynasty.

Codes

(a) I and II (b) II and III

(c) Both II and IV (d) All of these

38. Match the following.

List I (Religion)	List II (Religious texts)
A. Islam	1. Agama
B. Hinduism	2. Tripitakas
C. Buddhism	3. Vedas
D. Jainism	4. Shariyat

Codes

	A	B	C	D		A	B	C	D
(a)	4	3	2	1	(b)	2	3	1	4
(c)	1	2	4	3	(d)	3	1	4	2

39. Identify the site of Indus Valley Civilisation marked as A which is known as the first urban culture in India in the below map.

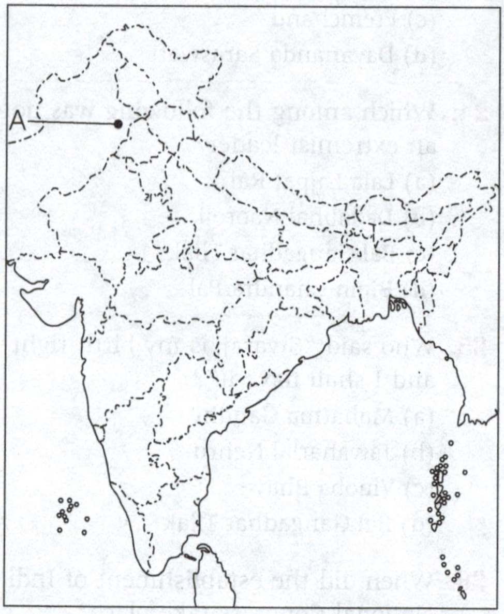

(a) Harappa (b) Mohenjodaro

(c) Lothal (d) Kalibangan

40. Read the following statements and select the correct option.

I. The Tripartite struggle was among the Palas, Pratiharas and Rashtrakutas rulers.

II. Chola Empire ruled the Western part of Indian sub-continent.

III. Vasco da Gama was a Portuguese explorer.

IV. Guru Arjan Dev was the founder of Sikhism.

Codes

(a) I and II (b) II and IV

(c) I and III (d) None of these

41. Identify the historical personality with the help of the information given below.

- He is also known as Tiger of Mysore.
- His father was Hyder Ali, the ruler of Mysore Kingdom in Southern India.

(a) Quli Qutb Shah (b) Tipu Sultan
(c) Sher Shah Suri (d) Adil Shah

42. Match the following.

	List II		List II
A.	Battle of Haldighati	1.	Prithviraj Chauhan and Mohammad Ghori
B.	Battle of Talikota	2.	Sher Shah Suri and Humayun
C.	Battle of Chausa	3.	Vijayanagara Empire and Deccan Sultanate
D.	Battle of Tarain	4.	Maharana Pratap and Akbar

Codes

	A	B	C	D
(a)	2	1	4	3
(b)	4	3	2	1
(c)	1	2	3	4
(d)	4	2	1	3

43. Identify the personality related to Bhakti Movement in India with the help of the information given below.

- He was a 15th century Indian mystic poet and saint.
- He is known to had written Bijak and Granthawali.

(a) Kabir
(b) Ravidas
(c) Ramanuja
(d) Chaitanya

Darken your choice with HB Pencil

1. a b c d	9. a b c d	17. a b c d	25. a b c d	33. a b c d	41. a b c d
2. a b c d	10. a b c d	18. a b c d	26. a b c d	34. a b c d	42. a b c d
3. a b c d	11. a b c d	19. a b c d	27. a b c d	35. a b c d	43. a b c d
4. a b c d	12. a b c d	20. a b c d	28. a b c d	36. a b c d	
5. a b c d	13. a b c d	21. a b c d	29. a b c d	37. a b c d	
6. a b c d	14. a b c d	22. a b c d	30. a b c d	38. a b c d	
7. a b c d	15. a b c d	23. a b c d	31. a b c d	39. a b c d	
8. a b c d	16. a b c d	24. a b c d	32. a b c d	40. a b c d	

Chapter 02

Tribal Movement in India

MCQs 1 Mark Questions

1. Which of the following tribes was associated with Pagal Panthis Movement?
   (a) Hajong tribes (b) Bodo tribes
   (c) Deori tribes (d) Konyak tribes

2. Who was the leader of Munda Rebellion?
   (a) Birsa Munda (b) Raghav Munda
   (c) Kanhu Munda (d) Sidhu Munda

3. What was the main region of Ho Revolt which was started in 1820-21?
   (a) Chota Nagpur (b) Bhagalpur
   (c) Haryana (d) Punjab

4. Identify the tribal group which was civilised by the Britishers.
   (a) Khond (b) Baiga
   (c) Naga (d) Santhal

5. Which of the following civil uprisings serves as the inspiration for novel 'Anandamath'?
   (a) Ahom Revolt
   (b) Sanyasi Revolt
   (c) Indigo Revolt
   (d) Santhal Uprising

6. In which state of India, the term 'Bewar' is used for shifting cultivation?
   (a) Nagaland (b) Bengal
   (c) Chhattisgarh (d) Madhya Pradesh

7. Which of the following tribal castes celebrated Diwali as condolence?
   (a) Sahariya (b) Tharu
   (c) Bhotiya (d) Pahariya

8. Who was the founder of Kuka Movement to restore Sikh rule over Punjab?
   (a) Baba Ram Singh
   (b) Bhagat Jawahar Mal
   (c) Lala Lajpat Rai
   (d) Kamal Khan Gakkhar

9. Who used the word 'Adivasi' for the first time to refer the tribal people of India?
   (a) Mahatma Gandhi (b) Thakkar Bappa
   (c) Jyotiba Phule (d) BR Ambedkar

10. Identify the incorrectly matched pair.
    (a) Kuka Movement – Bhagat Jawahar Mal
    (b) Wahabi Movement – Syed Ahmad
    (c) Ahoms' Revolt – Gomdhar Konwar
    (d) None of the above

11. Which of the following activities was practiced by Gaddi tribes of Himachal Pradesh?
    (a) Shifting cultivation (b) Animal rearing
    (c) Horticulture (d) Jhum cultivation

12. Identify the famous personality who was considered as 'Dharti Aaba' or Father of the 'land' by his followers.
    (a) Sidhu (b) Kanhu
    (c) Birsa Munda (d) Veer Narain

13. Complete the given analogy.
Khasi Uprising : North-East :: Bhil Revolt : ?
(a) Western Ghats
(b) Eastern Ghats
(c) Central India
(d) Southern India

14. Which of the following uprisings/rebellions is also known as Ulgulan (great commotion)?
(a) Ramosi Uprising
(b) Munda Uprising/Rebellion
(c) Santhal Rebellion
(d) Kol Uprising

15. The 'Tebhaga' movement of 1946 is associated with which among the following states of India?
(a) Andhra Pradesh
(b) West Bengal
(c) Bihar
(d) Odisha

MCQs 2 Marks Questions

16. Match the following.

List I (Tribal Group)	List II (Associated With)
A. Khonds	1. Hunting-gathering
B. Labadis	2. Cattle herding
C. Bakarwal	3. Rearing of goats
D. Santhal	4. Settled agriculture

Codes

	A	B	C	D		A	B	C	D
(a)	1	2	3	4	(b)	2	3	4	1
(c)	2	4	1	3	(d)	3	1	4	3

17. Which of the following statements about Santhals revolts is/are correct?
I. Santhals were from Rajmahal Hills.
II. Santhals rose up under Sidhu and Kanhu.

Codes
(a) Only I
(b) Only II
(c) Both I and II
(d) None of the above

18. Match the following.

List I (Revolts)	List II (Locations)
A. Moplah Revolt	1. Kerala
B. Pabna Revolt	2. Bengal
C. Eka Movement	3. Uttar Pradesh
D. Birsa Munda Revolt	4. Jharkhand

Codes

	A	B	C	D
(a)	1	3	4	2
(b)	2	3	4	1
(c)	1	2	3	4
(d)	3	4	1	2

19. Which of the following statements is/are correct?
I. Ramosi Uprising was associated with Ramosi tribals of Western Ghats.
II. Bhil Uprising in the Western Ghats organised under Govind Guru to fight for Bhil Raj.

Codes
(a) Only I
(b) Only II
(c) Both I and II
(d) None of the above

20. There are two statements marked as Assertion (A) and Reason (R). Mark your answer as per the codes given below.

Assertion (A) Pahariyas' Rebellion was led by Raja Jagannath.

Reason (R) Raja Jagannath led Pahariyas of Rajmahal Hills against British expansion on their land.

Codes

(a) Both A and R are true and R is the correct explanation of A

(b) Both A and R are true, but R is not the correct explanation of A

(c) A is true, but R is false

(d) A is false, but R is true

21. Read the following statements and identifies which ones are true (T) and which ones are false (F).

I. Bhil Rebellion was against the British feudalism and imperialism in Rajputana regions.

II. The Kol Uprising was a revolt of the Adivasi Kol people of Chota Nagpur region.

III. Sidhu and Kanhu were prominent leaders of Munda Rebellion.

Codes

	I	II	III		I	II	III
(a)	T	T	T	(b)	F	T	F
(c)	T	F	T	(d)	T	T	F

22.

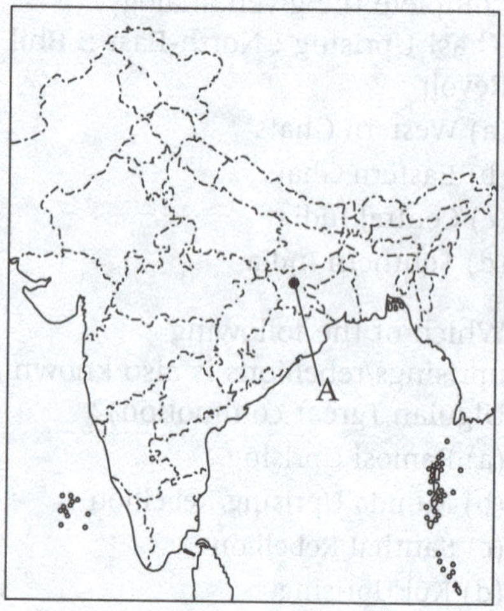

Identify the movement that was undertaken in the above marked region, which is also known as the Ulgulan Movement.

(a) Revolt of 1857 (b) Jaintia Rebellion
(c) Khond Uprising (d) Munda Rebellion

23. Identify the personality with the help of description given below.

- He fought against the British Policy of Expansionism and Interference in Gujarat.
- He led tribal revolt with a view to eliminate the British and establish Dharma-Raj.

(a) Sidhu (b) Joria Bhagath
(c) Birsa Munda (d) Tomma Sora

Darken your choice with HB Pencil

1.	ⓐ ⓑ ⓒ ⓓ	5.	ⓐ ⓑ ⓒ ⓓ	9.	ⓐ ⓑ ⓒ ⓓ	13.	ⓐ ⓑ ⓒ ⓓ	17.	ⓐ ⓑ ⓒ ⓓ	21.	ⓐ ⓑ ⓒ ⓓ
2.	ⓐ ⓑ ⓒ ⓓ	6.	ⓐ ⓑ ⓒ ⓓ	10.	ⓐ ⓑ ⓒ ⓓ	14.	ⓐ ⓑ ⓒ ⓓ	18.	ⓐ ⓑ ⓒ ⓓ	22.	ⓐ ⓑ ⓒ ⓓ
3.	ⓐ ⓑ ⓒ ⓓ	7.	ⓐ ⓑ ⓒ ⓓ	11.	ⓐ ⓑ ⓒ ⓓ	15.	ⓐ ⓑ ⓒ ⓓ	19.	ⓐ ⓑ ⓒ ⓓ	23.	ⓐ ⓑ ⓒ ⓓ
4.	ⓐ ⓑ ⓒ ⓓ	8.	ⓐ ⓑ ⓒ ⓓ	12.	ⓐ ⓑ ⓒ ⓓ	16.	ⓐ ⓑ ⓒ ⓓ	20.	ⓐ ⓑ ⓒ ⓓ		

Chapter

03

Social Reform Movement

MCQs 1 Mark Questions

1. In which of the following year, the Women's India Association (WIA) was formed?
(a) 1917 (b) 1918
(c) 1925 (d) 1926

2. .... was related with abolition of Sati practice in India.
(a) DK Karve
(b) Raja Ram Mohan Roy
(c) Mahadev Govind Ranade
(d) Ishwar Chandra Vidyasagar

3. Who among the following is associated with the Young Bengal Movement?
(a) Derozians (b) Mitra Bandhu
(c) Native Marriage Act (d) Bethune School

4. Which of the following Governor-Generals is associated with banning of Sati Pratha in India?
(a) Lord William Bentinck
(b) Warren Hastings
(c) Lord Canning
(d) Lord Cornwallis

5. Identify the name of the personality which is related to the establishment of Arya Samaj.
(a) Swami Dayananda Saraswati
(b) Bipin Chandra Chatterjee
(c) Rabindranath Tagore
(d) Swami Vivekananda

6. Who among the following is called as the 'Father of Indian Renaissance'?
(a) Debendranath Tagore
(b) Raja Ram Mohan Roy
(c) Swami Vivekananda
(d) Dayananda Saraswati

7. Identify the incorrectly matched pair.

	Social Reformer		Associated with
(a)	Raja Ram Mohan Roy	–	Brahmo Samaj
(b)	Debendranath Tagore	–	Tattvabodhini Sabha
(c)	Jyotiba Phule	–	Satyashodhak Samaj
(d)	Dayananda Saraswati	–	Ramakrishna Movement

8. Which among the following movements was supported by Gandhiji?
(a) Temple Entry Movement
(b) Self-Respect Movement
(c) Radhaswami Movement
(d) Vokkaligara Sangha Movement

9. Name the social reformer who worked for the upliftment of women in Maharashtra.
(a) Jyotirao Phule
(b) Bal Gangadhar Tilak
(c) Gopal Krishna Gokhale
(d) Mahatma Gandhi

10. Who among the following was the first female teacher of India?
(a) Annie Besant
(b) Madam Bhikaji Cama
(c) Sarojini Naidu
(d) Savitribai Phule

11. When did the evil practice of Sati banned in India?
(a) 1828 (b) 1829
(c) 1818 (d) 1857

12. The Asiatic Society of Bengal was established by ....
(a) William Jones (b) Richard Wellesely
(c) Charles Metcalf (d) Thomas Macaulay

13. Who among the following was popularly known as 'Lokahitawadi'?
(a) Jyotiba Phule
(b) Pt Ishwar Chandra Vidyasagar
(c) Gopal Hari Deshmukh
(d) Mahadev Govind Ranade

14. Complete the given analogy.
Gulamgiri : Jyotiba Phule :: Annihilation of Caste : ?
(a) Dr BR Ambedkar
(b) Jawaharlal Nehru
(c) Mahatma Gandhi
(d) Dayananda Saraswati

15. Who started the Mohammedan Anglo-Oriental College (Aligarh University) at Aligarh in 1875?
(a) Muhammad Qasim Nanautavi
(b) Rashid Ahmad Gangohi
(c) Mirza Ghulam Ahmad
(d) Syed Ahmad Khan

16. Which of the following leaders authored the book 'Stripurushtulna'?
(a) Mahatma Gandhi (b) Jyotirao Phule
(c) Tarabai Shinde (d) Pandita Ramabai

17. The personality in the given picture is of Sir Syed Ahmad Khan. He was associated with which among the following movements?

(a) Aligarh Movement
(b) Young Bengal Movement
(c) Prarthana Samaj
(d) Satyashodhak Samaj

18. Identify the incorrectly matched pair.

	Rules/Act	Year
(a)	Hindu Succession Act	– 1956
(b)	Hindu Widows Remarriage Act	– 1856
(c)	Child Marriage Restraint Act	– 1929
(d)	Bengal Sati Regulation Act	– 1854

19. Which of the following social reformers was associated with Bhoodan (land gift) Movement?
(a) Keshab Chandra Sen
(b) BM Malabari
(c) Vinoba Bhave
(d) Baba Amte

20. The first Women's School was founded by whom among the following?
(a) Jyotiba Phule (b) Annie Besant
(c) Narayan Guru (d) DK Karve

21. Who among the following founded the Nirankari Movement?
(a) Baba Dayal Das (b) Baba Ram Singh
(c) Mahmud Hasan (d) Jagat Mithra

22. Which of the following leaders is also known as Periyar?
(a) EV Ramasamy
(b) Jyotirao Phule
(c) Veerasalingam Pantulu
(d) Ishwar Chandra Vidyasagar

MCQs 2 Marks Questions

23. Read the following statements and select the correct option.
I. Raja Ram Mohan Roy is popularly known as first "Modern Man of India".
II. Prarthana Samaj was founded by Atmaram Pandurang.

Codes
(a) Only I (b) Only II
(c) Both I and II (d) None of these

24. Read the following statements and select the correct option.
I. Annie Besant was a leading member of the Theosophical Society.
II. Young Bengal Movement was related to demanding the equal right for the backward castes.

Codes
(a) Only I (b) Only II
(c) Both I and II (d) None of these

25. Which of the following statements is/are correct?
I. The Calcutta Madrasah was established by Warren Hastings.
II. The Sanskrit College was established by Jonathan Duncan.
III. Fort William College was set up by Wellesley.

Codes
(a) Only I (b) II and III
(c) Only III (d) All of these

26. Which of the following pairs is/are correctly matched?

	Social Movement		Associated States
I.	Nair Movement		Bombay
II.	Ramakrishna Mission	–	Bengal
III.	Self-Respect Movement	–	Tamil Nadu
IV.	Arya Samaj Movement	–	Kerala

Codes
(a) Only I (b) I and III
(c) II and III (d) I, II, III and IV

27. Identify the following personality with the help of the information given below.
- He is known as the 'Father of the Dravidian Movement'.
- He was well-known to have started the Self-Respect Movement.

(a) EV Ramasamy
(b) Gopal Hari Deshmukh
(c) Mahadev Govind Ranade
(d) Ishwar Chandra Vidyasagar

Darken your choice with HB Pencil

1. ⓐ ⓑ ⓒ ⓓ	6. ⓐ ⓑ ⓒ ⓓ	11. ⓐ ⓑ ⓒ ⓓ	16. ⓐ ⓑ ⓒ ⓓ	21. ⓐ ⓑ ⓒ ⓓ	26. ⓐ ⓑ ⓒ ⓓ
2. ⓐ ⓑ ⓒ ⓓ	7. ⓐ ⓑ ⓒ ⓓ	12. ⓐ ⓑ ⓒ ⓓ	17. ⓐ ⓑ ⓒ ⓓ	22. ⓐ ⓑ ⓒ ⓓ	27. ⓐ ⓑ ⓒ ⓓ
3. ⓐ ⓑ ⓒ ⓓ	8. ⓐ ⓑ ⓒ ⓓ	13. ⓐ ⓑ ⓒ ⓓ	18. ⓐ ⓑ ⓒ ⓓ	23. ⓐ ⓑ ⓒ ⓓ	
4. ⓐ ⓑ ⓒ ⓓ	9. ⓐ ⓑ ⓒ ⓓ	14. ⓐ ⓑ ⓒ ⓓ	19. ⓐ ⓑ ⓒ ⓓ	24. ⓐ ⓑ ⓒ ⓓ	
5. ⓐ ⓑ ⓒ ⓓ	10. ⓐ ⓑ ⓒ ⓓ	15. ⓐ ⓑ ⓒ ⓓ	20. ⓐ ⓑ ⓒ ⓓ	25. ⓐ ⓑ ⓒ ⓓ	

Chapter 04

Continents and Oceans

MCQs 1 Mark Questions

1. Which of the following continents is also known as the 'Dark Continent'?
(a) Australia (b) Africa
(c) Antarctica (d) Europe

2. Complete the given analogy.
Smallest Continent : Australia :: Smallest Ocean : ?
(a) Arctic (b) Pacific
(c) Atlantic (d) Southern

3. Which of the following continents is termed as a 'Continent of Contrast'?
(a) Europe (b) Asia
(c) Australia (d) South America

4. The countries Sweden, Austria and Germany are located in which continent?
(a) Europe (b) Australia
(c) Asia (d) North America

5. Which of the following is not a continent?
(a) Africa (b) Russia
(c) Antarctica (d) Australia

6. Identify the continent which does not have a desert.
(a) Africa (b) Asia
(c) Europe (d) Australia

7. What percentage of the Earth's surface is covered by continents?
(a) 50 (b) 2 (c) 9 (d) 29

8. .... is the art and science of making maps and charts.
(a) Geography (b) Geology
(c) Cartography (d) Morphology

9. The continent through which the Equator, Tropic of Cancer and Tropic of Capricorn passes is ....
(a) Australia (b) Africa
(c) Asia (d) Europe

10. Which of the following is the most populous continent in the world?
(a) Africa (b) Asia
(c) Antarctica (d) South America

11. The Greenland belongs to which of the following continents?
(a) North America (b) Australia
(c) Europe (d) Asia

12. Mount Everest is located in which continent?
(a) Africa (b) Europe
(c) Asia (d) South America

13. There are total .... oceans in the world.
(a) 4 (b) 5 (c) 6 (d) 7

14. The term 'Ring of Fire' is associated with which of the following oceans?
(a) Arctic (b) Atlantic
(c) Indian (d) Pacific

15. The name of the ocean that lies between North America and Africa is...............
(a) Atlantic Ocean (b) Arctic Ocean
(c) Antarctic Ocean (d) Indian Ocean

16. The world's deepest point 'Mariana Trench' is located in which of the following oceans?
(a) Atlantic (b) Pacific
(c) Southern (d) Indian

17. The world's longest river Nile drains into the ....
(a) Dead Sea (b) Black Sea
(c) Mediterranean Sea (d) Red Sea

18. Black Sea is a part of which ocean?
(a) Atlantic (b) Arctic
(c) Pacific (d) Indian

19. Identify the hemisphere in which the Arctic Ocean is located.
(a) Western hemisphere
(b) Southern hemisphere
(c) Eastern hemisphere
(d) Northern hemisphere

20. Madagascar is an island nation located in .... Ocean.
(a) Indian (b) Arctic
(c) Antarctic (d) Pacific

21. Which of the following is an 'S' shaped Ocean?
(a) Indian (b) Pacific
(c) Atlantic (d) Southern

22. The .... Ocean is the largest and deepest of the world ocean basins.
(a) Antarctic (b) Indian
(c) Pacific (d) Southern

MCQs 2 Marks Questions

23. Match the following.

List I (Continents)	**List II** (Countries)
A. Asia	1. Switzerland
B. Africa	2. Argentina
C. Europe	3. Bhutan
D. South America	4. Sudan

Codes

	A	B	C	D		A	B	C	D
(a)	3	4	1	2	(b)	4	1	2	3
(c)	1	2	3	4	(d)	4	3	2	1

24. Read the following statements and select the correct option.
I. Antarctica is the only continent with no permanent human habitation.
II. North America lies in the Southern ocean.

Codes
(a) Only I (b) Only II
(c) Both I and II (d) None of these

25. Which of the following statements is/are correct?
I. Australia is also known as Land of Kangaroos.
II. Australian continent is also known as Oceania.

Codes
(a) Only I (b) Only II
(c) Both I and II (d) None of these

26. Match the following.

List I (Oceans)	**List II** (Associated Seas)
A. Atlantic Ocean	1. Arabian Sea
B. Pacific Ocean	2. Caribbean Sea
C. Indian Ocean	3. South China Sea

Codes

	A	B	C		A	B	C
(a)	2	3	1	(b)	1	2	3
(c)	2	1	3	(d)	3	1	2

27. Read the following statements and select the correct option.

I. Antarctica is the only continent which is fully covered with ice.

II. Indian Ocean is the only ocean named after a country.

Codes

(a) Only I
(b) Only II
(c) Both I and II
(d) None of the above

28. Read the following statements and identifies which ones are true (T) and which ones are false (F).

I. Antarctica is known as the white continent.

II. North American continent is also known as the New World.

III. Atlantic Ocean is the world's saltiest ocean.

IV. Indian Ocean is the world's warmest ocean.

Codes

	I	II	III	IV		I	II	III	IV
(a)	T	T	T	T	(b)	F	T	F	T
(c)	T	F	T	F	(d)	F	F	F	F

29. There are two statements marked as Assertion (A) and Reason (R). Mark your answer as per the codes given below.

Assertion (A) Antarctic Ocean is also known as Southern Ocean.

Reason (R) Antarctic is permanently covered with ice.

Codes

(a) Both A and R are true and R is the correct explanation of A
(b) Both A and R are true, but R is not the correct explanation of A
(c) A is true, but R is false
(d) A is false, but R is true

30. Identify the name of the continent with the help of the given statements.

- The country of Japan lies on this continent.
- It is a part of Eurasian Supercontinent

(a) Asia (b) Africa
(c) Australia (d) Europe

Darken your choice with HB Pencil

1.	ⓐ ⓑ ⓒ ⓓ	6.	ⓐ ⓑ ⓒ ⓓ	11.	ⓐ ⓑ ⓒ ⓓ	16.	ⓐ ⓑ ⓒ ⓓ	21.	ⓐ ⓑ ⓒ ⓓ	26.	ⓐ ⓑ ⓒ ⓓ
2.	ⓐ ⓑ ⓒ ⓓ	7.	ⓐ ⓑ ⓒ ⓓ	12.	ⓐ ⓑ ⓒ ⓓ	17.	ⓐ ⓑ ⓒ ⓓ	22.	ⓐ ⓑ ⓒ ⓓ	27.	ⓐ ⓑ ⓒ ⓓ
3.	ⓐ ⓑ ⓒ ⓓ	8.	ⓐ ⓑ ⓒ ⓓ	13.	ⓐ ⓑ ⓒ ⓓ	18.	ⓐ ⓑ ⓒ ⓓ	23.	ⓐ ⓑ ⓒ ⓓ	28.	ⓐ ⓑ ⓒ ⓓ
4.	ⓐ ⓑ ⓒ ⓓ	9.	ⓐ ⓑ ⓒ ⓓ	14.	ⓐ ⓑ ⓒ ⓓ	19.	ⓐ ⓑ ⓒ ⓓ	24.	ⓐ ⓑ ⓒ ⓓ	29.	ⓐ ⓑ ⓒ ⓓ
5.	ⓐ ⓑ ⓒ ⓓ	10.	ⓐ ⓑ ⓒ ⓓ	15.	ⓐ ⓑ ⓒ ⓓ	20.	ⓐ ⓑ ⓒ ⓓ	25.	ⓐ ⓑ ⓒ ⓓ	30.	ⓐ ⓑ ⓒ ⓓ

Chapter 05

Natural Resources

MCQs 1 Mark Questions

1. What is the process of extracting useful minerals from the surface of the Earth including the sea called?
(a) Mining (b) Drilling
(c) Loading (d) Mapping

2. Identify the state which has the largest Gold reserve in India.
(a) Kerala (b) Tamil Nadu
(c) Odisha (d) Karnataka

3. Which of the following is considered as best quality coal?
(a) Peat
(b) Anthracite
(c) Lignite
(d) Bituminous

4. The term 'hydrosphere' is related to the ....
(a) hydrogen (b) landmass
(c) air (d) water

5. Which of the following factors is not involved in the process of water cycle?
(a) Transpiration
(b) Evaporation
(c) Precipitation
(d) Transportation

6. .... has the largest iron ore deposit in the world.
(a) Australia (b) Brazil
(c) India (d) China

7. Which of the following is not a greenhouse gas?
(a) Methane
(b) Carbon dioxide
(c) Oxygen
(d) Carbon monoxide

8. Identify the type of energy obtained in the image given below.

(a) Solar energy
(b) Geothermal energy
(c) Biogas energy
(d) Tidal energy

9. Which of the following is also known as 'Black Gold'?
(a) Diesel (b) Coal
(c) Petroleum (d) Natural gas

10. .... is also called as 'Buried Sunshine'.

(a) Coal (b) Gold
(c) Diamond (d) Copper

11. Identify the incorrectly matched pair.

(a) Humus – Soil structure
(b) Planting trees – Deforestation
(c) Ozone layer – Stratosphere
(d) Air pollution – Acid rain

12. Which of the following is an abiotic component of nature?

(a) Plants (b) Animals
(c) Microbes (d) Sunlight

13. Heat energy obtained from the Earth is called ....

(a) tidal energy
(b) geothermal energy
(c) solar energy
(d) nuclear energy

14. Identify the incorrectly matched pair.

	Resouces		Types
(a)	Solar energy	–	Non-conventional source of energy
(b)	Crude oil	–	Renewable energy
(c)	Wind energy	–	Non-conventional source of energy
(d)	Natural gas	–	Non-renewable energy

15. Which of the following countries is the leading producer of copper in the world?

(a) Chile (b) Sudan
(c) Australia (d) USA

16. Which one of the following movements was carried out for the conservation of forests and the environment?

(a) Forest Movement
(b) Ganga Action Plan
(c) Tehri Andolan
(d) Chipko Andolan

17. Complete the given analogy.

Renewable resource : Tidal energy : : Non-renewable resource : ?

(a) Solar energy
(b) Geothermal energy
(c) Wind energy
(d) Coal

MCQs 2 Marks Questions

18. Which of the following statements is/are correct?

I. Methane is a major biogas.
II. Deforestation reduces the chance of rainfall.

Codes

(a) Only I (b) Only II
(c) Both I and II (d) None of these

19. Identify the name of the power generating system with the help of the information given below.

- Norway was the first country to develop this system.
- It is a renewable source of energy that generates power by using a dam or diversion structure to alter the natural flow of a river or other body of water.

(a) Nuclear power (b) Hydel power
(c) Solar power (d) Geothermal power

20. Consider the following statements and choose the correct option.

I. Australia is the largest producer of the bauxite in the world.
II. Coal, petroleum and natural gases are also known as fossil fuels.
III. Switzerland has no known mineral deposits in it.

Codes

(a) I and II (b) II and III
(c) I and III (d) All of these

21. Read the following statements and select the correct option.

I. Electricity generated from coal is called Thermal Power.

II. China is the leading producer of coal in the world.

III. The use of CNG causes more pollution than petroleum and diesel.

IV. Nuclear power energy is obtained from geothermal energy.

Codes

(a) I and II (b) I, III and IV

(c) II and IV (d) None of these

22. Match the following.

List I (Spheres)	List II (Component)
A. Hydrosphere	1. Oceans and Rivers
B. Lithosphere	2. Crust
C. Stratosphere	3. Ozone
D. Biosphere	4. Existence of Life

Codes

	A	B	C	D
(a)	1	2	3	4
(b)	2	1	3	4
(c)	3	2	1	4
(d)	4	3	1	2

23. There are two statements marked as Assertion (A) and Reason (R). Mark your answer as per the codes given below.

Assertion (A) Human resources vary from natural and man-made resources because humans can use available resources to make other new productive output.

Reason (R) Technology is a human-made resource.

Codes

(a) Both A and R are true and R is the correct explanation of A

(b) Both A and R are true, but R is not the correct explanation of A

(c) A is true, but R is false

(d) A is false, but R is true

Darken your choice with HB Pencil

1.	ⓐ ⓑ ⓒ ⓓ	5.	ⓐ ⓑ ⓒ ⓓ	9.	ⓐ ⓑ ⓒ ⓓ	13.	ⓐ ⓑ ⓒ ⓓ	17.	ⓐ ⓑ ⓒ ⓓ	21.	ⓐ ⓑ ⓒ ⓓ
2.	ⓐ ⓑ ⓒ ⓓ	6.	ⓐ ⓑ ⓒ ⓓ	10.	ⓐ ⓑ ⓒ ⓓ	14.	ⓐ ⓑ ⓒ ⓓ	18.	ⓐ ⓑ ⓒ ⓓ	22.	ⓐ ⓑ ⓒ ⓓ
3.	ⓐ ⓑ ⓒ ⓓ	7.	ⓐ ⓑ ⓒ ⓓ	11.	ⓐ ⓑ ⓒ ⓓ	15.	ⓐ ⓑ ⓒ ⓓ	19.	ⓐ ⓑ ⓒ ⓓ	23.	ⓐ ⓑ ⓒ ⓓ
4.	ⓐ ⓑ ⓒ ⓓ	8.	ⓐ ⓑ ⓒ ⓓ	12.	ⓐ ⓑ ⓒ ⓓ	16.	ⓐ ⓑ ⓒ ⓓ	20.	ⓐ ⓑ ⓒ ⓓ		

Chapter 06

Vegetation and Wildlife

MCQs 1 Mark Questions

1. Which forest are called taiga forests?
   (a) Tropical Deciduous Forests
   (b) Tropical Rainforests
   (c) Tropical Evergreen Forests
   (d) Coniferous Forests

2. Tropical Thorn Forests and Scrubs can be found in which of the following states of India?
   (a) Chhattisgarh (b) Rajasthan
   (c) Madhya Pradesh (d) Odisha

3. Which of the following states of India has least forest cover?
   (a) Rajasthan (b) Haryana
   (c) Punjab (d) Odisha

4. The Manas National Park is located in the state of ....
   (a) Assam (b) Sikkim
   (c) Odisha (d) West Bengal

5. Oak, pine, eucalyptus trees are found in ....
   (a) Temperate Evergreen Forests
   (b) Tropical Deciduous Forests
   (c) Temperate Deciduous Forests
   (d) Tropical Evergreen Forests

6. In which of the following forests teak is a major species of tree?
   (a) Tropical Moist Deciduous Forests
   (b) Tropical Rainforests
   (c) Tropical Thorn and Scrub Forests
   (d) Temperate Forest with Grasslands

7. One-horned rhinoceroses can be found naturally in the state of ....
   (a) Gujarat (b) Bihar
   (c) West Bengal (d) Assam

8. Who among the following are considered as a vital cleanser of the environment?
   (a) Snake (b) Crow
   (c) Vultures (d) Tiger

9. Identify the incorrectly matched pair.
   (a) Tropical Evergreen Forests – Brazil
   (b) Coniferous Forests – Gujarat
   (c) Grasslands – South America
   (d) Tundra Vegetation – Polar Region

10. Complete the given analogy.
    Madumalai National Park : Tamil Nadu :: Keoladeo National Park : ?
    (a) Meghalaya (b) Nagaland
    (c) Rajasthan (d) Telangana

11. Which type of vegetation grows in saline areas?
    (a) Evergreen Forests (b) Mangrove Forests
    (c) Deciduous Forests (d) Mountain Forests

12. The major cultivation of spices can be found in which of the following regions of India?
(a) Kerala
(b) Eastern Ghats
(c) Jammu and Kashmir
(d) Rajasthan

13. Complete the given analogy.
Renuka Wetland : Himachal Pradesh :: Sundarban : ?
(a) Himachal Pradesh (b) Madhya Pradesh
(c) Tamil Nadu (d) West Bengal

14. Which among the following forests are known as lungs of the world?
(a) Tropical Evergreen Forests
(b) Coniferous Forests
(c) Temperate Deciduous Forests
(d) Tropical Deciduous Forests

15. What is the full form of CITES ?
(a) Convention on International Trade in Endangered Species of Wild Fauna and Flora
(b) Convention on International Trade in Endemic Species
(c) Convention on International Trade in Invasive Alien Species
(d) None of the above

16. Gir National Park is situated in ....
(a) Madhya Pradesh (b) Assam
(c) Chhattisgarh (d) Gujarat

17. Which of the following animals is the national aquatic animal of India?

(a)  (b) 

(c)  (d) 

18. Who among the following releases the Red List of Endangered Species?
(a) IUCN (b) UNEP
(c) CITES (d) UNFCC

19. The highest degree of protection to the flora and fauna is provided in which of the following protected areas?
(a) Bird Sanctuary
(b) National Park
(c) Wildlife Sanctuary
(d) Biosphere Reserve

20. Identify the state of India in which the Kanha National Park is located.
(a) Assam (b) Madhya Pradesh
(c) Maharashtra (d) Rajasthan

21. Which among the following is the world's only floating National Park?
(a) Similipal National Park
(b) Manas National Park
(c) Keibul-Lamjao National Park
(d) Keoladeo Ghana National Park

MCQs 2 Marks Questions

22. Identify the national park which is regarded as one of the finest wildlife refuges in the world shown in the given map.

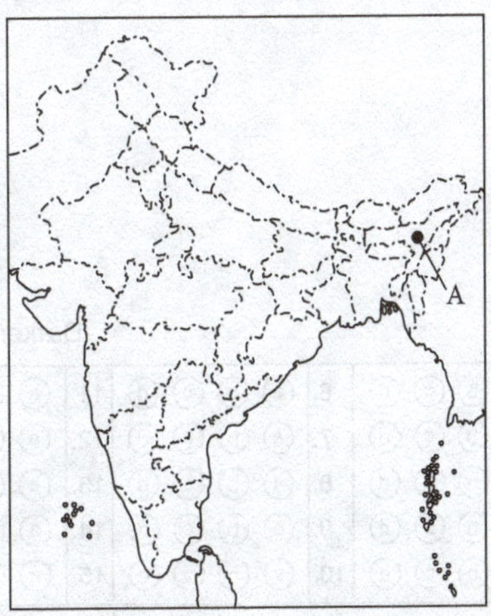

(a) Manas National Park
(b) Kaziranga National Park
(c) Rajiv Gandhi Orang National Park
(d) Dibru-Saikhowa National Park

23. Identify the forest with the help of the information given below.

- These forests have tall, softwood and evergreen trees.
- Chir, pine and cedar are important trees of these forests.

(a) Coniferous (b) Deciduous
(c) Mediterranean (d) Temperate

24. Match the following.

List I (State)	List II (Protected areas)
A. Madhya Pradesh	1. Bandipur National Park
B. Rajasthan	2. Bandhavgarh National Park
C. Karnataka	3. Periyar National Park
D. Kerala	4. Ranthambore National Park

Codes

	A	B	C	D
(a)	2	4	1	3
(b)	1	2	3	4
(c)	3	4	2	1
(d)	2	1	3	4

25. Match the following.

List I (Forests)	List II (Famous Trees)
A. Evergreen	1. Mahogany
B. Deciduous	2. Oak
C. Coniferous	3. Fir
D. Temperate	4. Pine

Codes

	A	B	C	D
(a)	1	2	4	3
(b)	3	4	1	2
(c)	2	1	4	3
(d)	4	1	3	2

26. Which among the following statements are incorrect?

I. Manas National Park is located in two districts of Assam and it is situated at the foothills of the Himalayas.
II. Tropical Evergreen Forests are found in the Western Ghats and the island groups of Lakshadweep, Andaman and Nicobar.
III. Acacias, palms, euphorbias and cacti are the main plant species of Tropical Thorn Forests and Scrubs.

Codes

(a) I and II (b) II and IV
(c) I, II and III (d) None of these

Darken your choice with HB Pencil

1.	ⓐ ⓑ ⓒ ⓓ	6.	ⓐ ⓑ ⓒ ⓓ	11.	ⓐ ⓑ ⓒ ⓓ	16.	ⓐ ⓑ ⓒ ⓓ	21.	ⓐ ⓑ ⓒ ⓓ	26.	ⓐ ⓑ ⓒ ⓓ
2.	ⓐ ⓑ ⓒ ⓓ	7.	ⓐ ⓑ ⓒ ⓓ	12.	ⓐ ⓑ ⓒ ⓓ	17.	ⓐ ⓑ ⓒ ⓓ	22.	ⓐ ⓑ ⓒ ⓓ		
3.	ⓐ ⓑ ⓒ ⓓ	8.	ⓐ ⓑ ⓒ ⓓ	13.	ⓐ ⓑ ⓒ ⓓ	18.	ⓐ ⓑ ⓒ ⓓ	23.	ⓐ ⓑ ⓒ ⓓ		
4.	ⓐ ⓑ ⓒ ⓓ	9.	ⓐ ⓑ ⓒ ⓓ	14.	ⓐ ⓑ ⓒ ⓓ	19.	ⓐ ⓑ ⓒ ⓓ	24.	ⓐ ⓑ ⓒ ⓓ		
5.	ⓐ ⓑ ⓒ ⓓ	10.	ⓐ ⓑ ⓒ ⓓ	15.	ⓐ ⓑ ⓒ ⓓ	20.	ⓐ ⓑ ⓒ ⓓ	25.	ⓐ ⓑ ⓒ ⓓ		

Chapter 07

Human Resource

MCQs 1 Mark Questions

1. The concentration of individuals in a specific geographic location is called ....
   (a) population outgrowth
   (b) population density
   (c) population migration
   (d) population change

2. Which term is used to define the average number of years of life a person can expect to live?
   (a) Life expectancy (b) Birth rate
   (c) Death rate (d) Growth rate

3. Complete the given analogy.
   High Population : Plains :: Low Population : ?
   (a) Rural areas
   (b) Metro cities
   (c) Deserts/ mountainous region
   (d) River banks

4. Complete the given analogy.
   Climate : Geographical factor :: Culture : ?
   (a) Natural factor (b) Social factor
   (c) Economic factor (d) Political factor

5. Which of the following countries is the most populous nation in the world?
   (a) USA (b) India
   (c) Brazil (d) Russia

6. Which of the following countries has slow growth rate of the population?
   (a) India (b) USA
   (c) England (d) Brazil

7. The process of long lasting development without impacting the environment negatively is called............... .
   (a) resource development
   (b) sustainable conservation
   (c) sustainable development
   (d) resource conservation

8. The productivity of a nation's human resources depends on which of the following factors?
   (a) Health (b) Technical skills
   (c) Literacy (d) All of these

9. What do understand by the term Census?
   (a) The process of counting the number of states in a country.
   (b) The process of counting total number of population in a country.
   (c) The process of counting total birth rates in a specific area.
   (d) The process of counting the literate population in a country.

10. The population of a region decreases when there is high ....
    (a) emigration (b) death rate
    (c) Both (a) and (b) (d) natural calamity

11. The population change is/ are caused by ....
(a) birth
(b) death
(c) migration
(d) All of the above

12. Which of the following ministries conducts the Census in India?
(a) Ministry of Health and Family Welfare
(b) Ministry of Home Affairs
(c) Ministry of Education
(d) Ministry of Skill Development and Entrepreneurship

13. The first Census of India was conducted in the year ....
(a) 1881 (b) 1886
(c) 1882 (d) 1818

14. Which of the following factors develop people as a resource?
(a) Health
(b) Education
(c) Skills
(d) All of the above

15. The Literacy Rate as per Census 2011 was ....
(a) 74% (b) 64%
(c) 80% (d) 55%

16. What is the full form of MGNREGA?
(a) Mahatma Gandhi National Rural Employment Guarantee Act
(b) Mahatma Gandhi New Rural Employment Government Act
(c) Mahatma Gandhi Natural Rural Employment Guarantee Act
(d) Mahatma Gandhi New Rural Employment Government Administration

17. The condition in which a person is capable of working, actively seeking work, but unable to find any work is called ....
(a) unemployment (b) employment
(c) employee (d) employer

18. Which of the following factors is/are responsible for the distribution of population?
(a) Landform (b) Topography
(c) Climate (d) All of these

MCQs 2 Marks Questions

19. Read the following statements and choose the correct option.
I. The population pyramid gives information about the age and sex of population.
II. The primary sector generates maximum employment in India.
III. The process through which individuals become permanent residents or citizens of another country is called immigration.

Codes
(a) I and II (b) II and III
(c) I and III (d) All of these

20. Read the following statements and choose the correct option.
I. The number of deaths per 1,000 people refers to death rate.
II. The number of maternal deaths during a given time period per 100,000 live births is called maternal mortality ratio.

Codes
(a) Only I (b) Only II
(c) Both I and II (d) None of these

21. Match the following.

List I (Parameter)		List II (Defination)
A. Population	1.	The whole number of people or inhabitants in a country
B. Emigration	2.	Movement of people in and out of an area
C. Migration	3.	When a person leaves a country

Codes

	A	B	C
(a)	1	3	2
(b)	1	2	3
(c)	3	2	1
(d)	3	1	2

22. Which of the following statements are correct?

I. The full form of MMR is Maximum Mortality Ratio.

II. Ganga Plains is the most densely populated region of India.

III. The Metro cities of India are overpopulated.

IV. Japan is the most youthful nation in the world.

Codes

(a) II and III

(b) I and II

(c) I, III and IV

(d) All of the above

23. Read the following statements and identifies which ones are true (T) and which ones are false (F).

I. The Maternal Mortality Rate (MMR) is the number of maternal death per 10,000 live births in a given year.

II. Birth rate is the number of live births per 1,000 persons in a year.

III. Migration is the movement of people across regions and territories.

Codes

	I	II	III		I	II	III
(a)	F	T	T	(b)	F	T	F
(c)	T	F	T	(d)	F	F	F

Darken your choice with HB Pencil

1.	ⓐ	ⓑ	ⓒ	ⓓ	**5.**	ⓐ	ⓑ	ⓒ	ⓓ	**9.**	ⓐ	ⓑ	ⓒ	ⓓ	**13.**	ⓐ	ⓑ	ⓒ	ⓓ	**17.**	ⓐ	ⓑ	ⓒ	ⓓ	**21.**	ⓐ	ⓑ	ⓒ	ⓓ
2.	ⓐ	ⓑ	ⓒ	ⓓ	**6.**	ⓐ	ⓑ	ⓒ	ⓓ	**10.**	ⓐ	ⓑ	ⓒ	ⓓ	**14.**	ⓐ	ⓑ	ⓒ	ⓓ	**18.**	ⓐ	ⓑ	ⓒ	ⓓ	**22.**	ⓐ	ⓑ	ⓒ	ⓓ
3.	ⓐ	ⓑ	ⓒ	ⓓ	**7.**	ⓐ	ⓑ	ⓒ	ⓓ	**11.**	ⓐ	ⓑ	ⓒ	ⓓ	**15.**	ⓐ	ⓑ	ⓒ	ⓓ	**19.**	ⓐ	ⓑ	ⓒ	ⓓ	**23.**	ⓐ	ⓑ	ⓒ	ⓓ
4.	ⓐ	ⓑ	ⓒ	ⓓ	**8.**	ⓐ	ⓑ	ⓒ	ⓓ	**12.**	ⓐ	ⓑ	ⓒ	ⓓ	**16.**	ⓐ	ⓑ	ⓒ	ⓓ	**20.**	ⓐ	ⓑ	ⓒ	ⓓ					

Chapter 08

Agriculture

MCQs 1 Mark Questions

1. The term 'pisciculture' is related to which of the following?
(a) Agriculture
(b) Rearing silkworms
(c) Cultivation of cotton
(d) Breeding of fish

2. What does the term 'arable land' used for?
(a) Crop cultivation (b) Irrigated land
(c) Barren land (d) Fallow land

3. The term 'sericulture' is related to which of the following options?
(a) Commercial rearing of silkworms
(b) Sugarcane cultivation
(c) Cultivation of jute
(d) Growing ornamental plants

4. Growing of two crops in a definite row proportion on the same piece of land is called ....
(a) parallel cropping
(b) inter cropping
(c) mixed cropping
(d) mono cropping

5. Which of the following elements is a part of organic farming?
(a) Insecticides (b) Natural manure
(c) Pesticides (d) Chemical fertilises

6. .... agriculture occurs when farmers grow food crops to meet the needs of themselves and their families on smallholdings.
(a) Subsistence (b) Commercial
(c) Organic (d) Cooperative

7. Crops which are grown primarily as food for animals are called ....
(a) fibre crop (b) ornamental crop
(c) cash crop (d) fodder crop

8. Which type of farming involves both the growing of crops and the raising of livestock?
(a) Natural farming
(b) Subsistence farming
(c) Organic farming
(d) Mixed farming

9. Which of the following soils is also known as 'regur soil'?
(a) Black soil (b) Alluvial soil
(c) Laterite soil (d) Red soil

10. The crop which is a water intensive crop is ....
(a) wheat (b) sugarcane
(c) cotton (d) pulses

11. Cultivation of grapes is called as ....
(a) sericulture (b) viticulture
(c) floriculture (d) horticulture

12. Which of the following states is the largest producer of sugarcane in India?
(a) Madhya Pradesh
(b) Uttar Pradesh
(c) Arunachal Pradesh
(d) Himachal Pradesh

13. Which of the following crops are also known as coarse grains?
(a) Millets (b) Wheat
(c) Rice (d) Jute

14. Identify the country which is the largest producer of rice in the world.
(a) India (b) China
(c) Bangladesh (d) USA

15. In which type of farming, the machines are used on a large scale?
(a) Subsistence farming
(b) Shifting cultivation
(c) Mixed farming
(d) Commercial farming

16. In agriculture, the term horticulture refers to........
(a) growing of fruits and vegetables
(b) primitive farming
(c) subsistence farming
(d) tea and coffee plantations

17. .... is also known as golden fibre.
(a) Jute (b) Cotton
(c) Sunflower (d) Pulses

18. What is the meaning of food security?
(a) Availability and access of food
(b) Food preservation
(c) Food import
(d) Packaging of food

19. Complete the given analogy.
Maize : Kharif crop : : Watermelon : ?
(a) Rabi crop (b) Kharif crop
(c) Zaid crop (d) None of these

20. White Revolution is related to which of the following?
(a) Egg (b) Milk (c) Rice (d) Cotton

21. Identify the crop that requires frost free environment to grow.
(a) Rice (b) Wheat
(c) Sugarcane (d) Cotton

22. Wheat is a .... crop and a staple diet of the Indian sub-continent.
(a) kharif (b) rabi
(c) zaid (d) None of these

23. Operation Flood is related to ....
(a) self sufficiency in milk and dairy production.
(b) importing petroleum and natural gas.
(c) safety drills related to flood.
(d) river management system.

24. Cereals, coffee, cocoa, cotton and tobacco are examples of ....
(a) cash crops (b) ornamental crops
(c) fodder crops (d) fibre crops

25. What is the rearing, breeding and management of honey bees for the production of honey and wax called?
(a) apiculture (b) sericulture
(c) horticulture (d) floriculture

26. 'Truck farming' is associated with which of the following?
(a) Cultivation of vegetables
(b) Cotton cultivation
(c) Bulk production of millets
(d) None of the above

MCQs 2 Marks Questions

27. Which of the following are the soil replenishment methods?
I. Crop rotation
II. Vermicomposting

III. Manure use
IV. Growing of leguminous plants

Codes

(a) I and II (b) II and III
(c) I and III (d) All of these

28. Identify the soil with the help of the information given below.

- It is considered as the most fertile soil in India.
- It is formed by deposition of sediments carried by rivers and sea waves over many years.

(a) Black soil (b) Laterite soil
(c) Alluvial soil (d) Red soil

29. Match the following.

List I (Crops)	List II (Leading producer state)
A. Coffee	1. Rajasthan
B. Spices	2. Karnataka
C. Jute	3. Kerala
D. Millets	4. West Bengal

Codes

	A	B	C	D		A	B	C	D
(a)	1	2	3	4	(b)	2	3	4	1
(c)	4	3	2	1	(d)	3	1	4	2

30. There are two statements marked as Assertion (A) and Reason (R). Mark your answer as per the codes given below.

Assertion (A) Nomadic herding is practiced in the semi-arid and arid regions.

Reason (R) Nomadic herding takes place in response to climatic constraints and terrain.

Codes

(a) Both A and R are true and R is the correct explanation of A
(b) Both A and R are true, but R is not the correct explanation of A
(c) A is true, but R is false
(d) A is false, but R is true

31. Read the following statements and choose the correct option.

I. Alphonso, Dasheri and Chausa are the varities of Mangoes in India.
II. Tea plantations are usually grown on hill slopes.

Codes

(a) Only I (b) Both I and II
(c) Only II (d) None of these

32. Read the following statements and choose the correct option.

I. Silver Fibre Revolution is related to cotton production.
II. Black Revolution is related to coal.
III. The Blue Revolution is related to fish production.
IV. Green Revolution is related to food grains production in India.

Codes

(a) I and III (b) II and III
(c) I, III and IV (d) All of these

Darken your choice with HB Pencil

1.	ⓐ ⓑ ⓒ ⓓ	7.	ⓐ ⓑ ⓒ ⓓ	13.	ⓐ ⓑ ⓒ ⓓ	19.	ⓐ ⓑ ⓒ ⓓ	25.	ⓐ ⓑ ⓒ ⓓ	31.	ⓐ ⓑ ⓒ ⓓ
2.	ⓐ ⓑ ⓒ ⓓ	8.	ⓐ ⓑ ⓒ ⓓ	14.	ⓐ ⓑ ⓒ ⓓ	20.	ⓐ ⓑ ⓒ ⓓ	26.	ⓐ ⓑ ⓒ ⓓ	32.	ⓐ ⓑ ⓒ ⓓ
3.	ⓐ ⓑ ⓒ ⓓ	9.	ⓐ ⓑ ⓒ ⓓ	15.	ⓐ ⓑ ⓒ ⓓ	21.	ⓐ ⓑ ⓒ ⓓ	27.	ⓐ ⓑ ⓒ ⓓ		
4.	ⓐ ⓑ ⓒ ⓓ	10.	ⓐ ⓑ ⓒ ⓓ	16.	ⓐ ⓑ ⓒ ⓓ	22.	ⓐ ⓑ ⓒ ⓓ	28.	ⓐ ⓑ ⓒ ⓓ		
5.	ⓐ ⓑ ⓒ ⓓ	11.	ⓐ ⓑ ⓒ ⓓ	17.	ⓐ ⓑ ⓒ ⓓ	23.	ⓐ ⓑ ⓒ ⓓ	29.	ⓐ ⓑ ⓒ ⓓ		
6.	ⓐ ⓑ ⓒ ⓓ	12.	ⓐ ⓑ ⓒ ⓓ	18.	ⓐ ⓑ ⓒ ⓓ	24.	ⓐ ⓑ ⓒ ⓓ	30.	ⓐ ⓑ ⓒ ⓓ		

Chapter 09

Industries in India

MCQs 1 Mark Questions

1. Which of the following industries is also known as manufacturing industries?
   (a) Primary industry
   (b) Secondary industry
   (c) Tertiary industry
   (d) None of the above

2. Where was the first steel plant set up in India?
   (a) Jamshedpur (b) Bokaro
   (c) Rourkela (d) Bhadravati

3. The primary sector of the economy is related to the .... sector.
   (a) mining
   (b) manufacturing
   (c) service
   (d) automobile

4. Complete the given analogy.
   Oil and gas extraction : Primary sector activity :: Health and social work : ?
   (a) Primary sector activity
   (b) Secondary sector activity
   (c) Tertiary sector activity
   (d) None of the above

5. The largest share of the Gross Domestic Product (GDP) comes from which sector in India?
   (a) Agriculture and allied sector
   (b) Manufacturing sector
   (c) Tertiary sector
   (d) Private sector

6. .... is concerned with information-based or knowledge-oriented products and services.
   (a) Primary industry
   (b) Secondary industry
   (c) Tertiary industry
   (d) Quaternary industry

7. Which of the following is/are a locational factors for an industry?
   (a) Transport
   (b) Land
   (c) Power
   (d) All of the above

8. An emerging industry is also known as ....
   (a) Sunset industry
   (b) Sunrise industry
   (c) Sunshine industry
   (d) Sunbath industry

9. Identify the name of the sector as shown in the image given below.

(a) Primary sector
(b) Secondary sector
(c) Tertiary sector
(d) None of the above

10. Which of the following cities is a major hub of 'Information Technology' (IT) industry in India?
(a) Chennai
(b) Gurugram
(c) Bengaluru
(d) Delhi

11. Which of the following Steel Plant is located in Chhattisgarh?
(a) Bhilai Steel Plant
(b) Bokaro Steel Plant
(c) Bastar Steel Plant
(d) None of the above

12. The .... are owned and operated by the producers or suppliers of raw materials, workers, etc.
(a) cooperative sector industries
(b) heavy industries
(c) light industries
(d) public sector companies

13. Where was the first successful textile mill established in India?
(a) Bombay
(b) Calcutta
(c) Surat
(d) Madras

14. The major cotton industries are located in the regions of ....
(a) Karnataka and Andhra Pradesh
(b) Maharashtra and Karnataka
(c) Maharashtra and Gujarat
(d) Gujarat and Rajasthan

15. Which of the following statements is correct?
(a) Rajasthan is the largest coal producing state in India.
(b) The state of Odisha is famous for its tea production worldwide.
(c) Karnataka is the largest producer of gold in India.
(d) The mining and quarrying activities are related to the secondary sector.

16. Complete the given analogy.
TISCO : Steel manufacturing :: BHEL : ?
(a) Heavy electricals
(b) Housings
(c) Gold manufacturing
(d) Ship and port activities

17. The industries related to paper, match, silk, lac, sports goods and handicrafts comes under the................. .
(a) mineral-based industries
(b) agro-based industries
(c) marine-based industries
(d) forest-based industries

18. .... is a type of business or manufacturing activity carried on in people's homes.
(a) Home industry
(b) Cottage industry
(c) Roof industry
(d) Small scale industry

19. Which of the following metals is called the backbone of the modern industry?
(a) Gold (b) Silver
(c) Aluminium (d) Steel

20. Which of the following statements is/are incorrect?
(a) Kanpur is famous for its leather industry in India.
(b) India is the largest producer of gold.
(c) Both (a) and (b)
(d) Cotton is a pure and not weight losing raw material.

21. TISCO was established in 1907 in the state of ....
(a) Odisha
(b) Jharkhand
(c) Uttar Pradesh
(d) Chhattisgarh

22. Identify the image related to government's initiative to boost the India's manufacturing sector.

(a) Make in India
(b) Digital India
(c) Swachh Bharat Mission
(d) None of the above

MCQs 2 Marks Questions

23. Consider the following statements and choose the correct option.
I. AMUL was established by Dr Verghese Kurien in Gujarat.
II. He is also known as Father of Indian Green Revolution.

Codes
(a) Only I
(b) Only II
(c) Both I and II
(d) None of the above

24. Read the following statements and choose the correct option.
I. SAIL is related to the steel manufacturing in India.
II. West Bengal is the largest jute producing state in India.
III. Mother Dairy is a cooperative society.
IV. Bengaluru is also known as the 'Silicon Valley of India'.

Codes
(a) I and II
(b) II and III
(c) I, II and IV
(d) All of the above

25. Match the following.

	List I (Industrial Plants)		List II (States)
A.	Narora Atomic Power Station	1.	Maharashtra
B.	Rourkela Steel Plant	2.	West Bengal
C.	Durgapur Steel Plant	3.	Odisha
D.	Tarapur Nuclear Power Station	4.	Uttar Pradesh

Codes

	A	B	C	D		A	B	C	D
(a)	4	3	2	1	(b)	3	1	4	2
(c)	2	3	4	1	(d)	1	2	3	4

26. Consider the following statements and choose the correct option.
I. India, China and Japan are important producer of cotton textile.
II. Ahmedabad city is also known as Manchester of India.
III. Firozabad in Uttar Pradesh is famous for its bangle industries.

Codes
(a) I and II
(b) II and III
(c) I and III
(d) All of these

27. Identify the crop with the help of the information given below.

- India is a leading producer of this crop.
- The crop related to this industry grows best in black soil.

(a) Jute
(b) Cotton
(c) Wheat
(d) Sugarcane

28. Read the following statements and choose the incorrect option.

I. Jamshedpur lies on the bank of river Yamuna.
II. Food processing is an example of mineral-based industry.
III. Garments and textile are related to water intensive industry.

Codes

(a) I and II
(b) I and III
(c) Only III
(d) All of the above

29. Read the following statements and identifies which ones are true (T) and which ones are false (F).

I. Iron made from iron ore is the product of mineral-based industry.
II. Small scale industries use lesser amount of capital and technology.
III. Production of automobiles and heavy machinery are large scale industries.

Codes

	I	II	III		I	II	III
(a)	T	T	T	(b)	F	F	F
(c)	F	T	F	(d)	T	F	T

Darken your choice with HB Pencil

1.	ⓐ ⓑ ⓒ ⓓ	6.	ⓐ ⓑ ⓒ ⓓ	11.	ⓐ ⓑ ⓒ ⓓ	16.	ⓐ ⓑ ⓒ ⓓ	21.	ⓐ ⓑ ⓒ ⓓ	26.	ⓐ ⓑ ⓒ ⓓ
2.	ⓐ ⓑ ⓒ ⓓ	7.	ⓐ ⓑ ⓒ ⓓ	12.	ⓐ ⓑ ⓒ ⓓ	17.	ⓐ ⓑ ⓒ ⓓ	22.	ⓐ ⓑ ⓒ ⓓ	27.	ⓐ ⓑ ⓒ ⓓ
3.	ⓐ ⓑ ⓒ ⓓ	8.	ⓐ ⓑ ⓒ ⓓ	13.	ⓐ ⓑ ⓒ ⓓ	18.	ⓐ ⓑ ⓒ ⓓ	23.	ⓐ ⓑ ⓒ ⓓ	28.	ⓐ ⓑ ⓒ ⓓ
4.	ⓐ ⓑ ⓒ ⓓ	9.	ⓐ ⓑ ⓒ ⓓ	14.	ⓐ ⓑ ⓒ ⓓ	19.	ⓐ ⓑ ⓒ ⓓ	24.	ⓐ ⓑ ⓒ ⓓ	29.	ⓐ ⓑ ⓒ ⓓ
5.	ⓐ ⓑ ⓒ ⓓ	10.	ⓐ ⓑ ⓒ ⓓ	15.	ⓐ ⓑ ⓒ ⓓ	20.	ⓐ ⓑ ⓒ ⓓ	25.	ⓐ ⓑ ⓒ ⓓ		

Chapter

10

Environment

MCQs 1 Mark Questions

1. Which of the following is an example of aquatic ecosytem?
(a) Desert (b) Pond
(c) Mountain (d) Plateau

2. The natural place of an organism is known as ....
(a) habitat (b) biosphere
(c) niche (d) habit

3. Which of the following parks is known as India's first 'Mixed World Heritage Site' of UNESCO?
(a) Khanchenjunga National Park
(b) Kuno National Park
(c) Gir National Park
(d) Kaziranga National Park

4. Which of the following is an artificial ecosystem?
(a) Forest (b) Pond
(c) Grasslands (d) Fields

5. Identify the personality related to the Narmada Bachao Andolan.
(a) Tulsi Gowda
(b) Medha Patekar
(c) Thimmakka
(d) Vandana Shiva

6. A wide variety of living organisms on the Earth is called ....
(a) biodiversity (b) population
(c) habitat (d) diversity

7. Identify the movement with the help of the image given below.

(a) Tehri Dam Movement
(b) Chipko Andolan
(c) Appiko Movement
(d) Narmada Bachao Andolan

8. Which of the following is an abiotic component of the environment?
(a) Plants (b) Animals
(c) Temperature (d) Microbes

9. Acid rain is a result of excess amount of ....
(a) CO_2
(b) NH_3
(c) SO_2 and NO_2
(d) carbon monoxide

10. What is an organism that regularly consumes a variety of material including plants, animals, algae and fungi called?

(a) Omnivorous (b) Herbivorous
(c) Carnivorous (d) None of these

11. Which of the following organisms has autotrophic mode of nutrition?

(a) Human (b) Plants
(c) Lion (d) Cats

12. The Silent Valley National Park is located in the state of ....

(a) Kerala (b) Karnataka
(c) Tamil Nadu (d) Andhra Pradesh

13. Which of the following is responsible for 'Green House Effect'?

(a) Nitrogen
(b) Carbon dioxide
(c) Carbon monoxide
(d) Nitrogen dioxide

14. The maximum biodiversity can be observed on ....

(a) desert
(b) polar region
(c) tropical region
(d) oceans

15. Which of the following is a renewable source of energy?

(a) Coal (b) Solar power
(c) Natural gas (d) Atomic power

16. .... is the process of removal of the top layer of soil and reducing the fertility.

(a) Soil erosion (b) Soil degradation
(c) Soil fertility (d) Soil mulching

17. Which among the following are the primary consumers?

(a) Carnivores (b) Herbivores
(c) Omnivores (d) Producers

18. Identify which among the following is not a component of human environment.

(a) Religion
(b) Community
(c) Natural Resources
(d) Culture

19. Which among the following comprises of biotic components of environment?

(a) Producers (b) Consumers
(c) Decomposers (d) All of these

20. Which among the following is not a part of tertiary consumers?

(a) Tiger (b) Lion
(c) Cheetah (d) Bacteria

21. The organisms depicted in given image are part of which among the following?

(a) Primary Consumers
(b) Secondary Consumers
(c) Tertiary Consumers
(d) Decomposers

22. Identify the major air pollutant(s) from the options given below.

(a) Carbon monoxide
(b) Sulphur dioxide
(c) Flourides smoke
(d) All of the above

23. Which among the following is/are the source(s) of radioactive pollution?

(a) Pollution from rays used in treatment
(b) Fuels used in atomic reactors
(c) Use of nuclear weapons
(d) All of the above

MCQs 2 Marks Questions

24. Match the following

List I (Types of Pollution)		List II (Sources)	
A.	Water Pollution	1.	Oil spill
B.	Soil Pollution	2.	Excretion in open fields
C.	Air Pollution	3.	Smog
D.	Noise Pollution	4.	Honking of vehicles

Codes

	A	B	C	D		A	B	C	D
(a)	1	2	3	4	(b)	2	1	4	3
(c)	3	2	4	1	(d)	4	3	1	2

25. Read the following statements and choose the correct option.

I. Hibernation helps to save energy among animals in winters.

II. The process of hibernation can be observed in bears and bats.

Codes

(a) Only I (b) Only II
(c) Both I and II (d) None of these

26. Read the following statements and identifies which ones are true (T) and which ones are false (F).

I. The thin layer of grainy substance covering the surface of the Earth is called soil.

II. Saline water is found in the forms of groundwater, water in rivers and lakes, and water vapour.

III. Water cycle is the process involved in the formation of rain.

Codes

	I	II	III		I	II	III
(a)	T	F	T	(b)	F	T	F
(c)	T	F	F	(d)	T	T	T

27. Read the following statements and choose the correct option.

I. The process of the clearing of the forested land is called afforestation.

II. Tourism and construction are one of the factors that led to pressure on land and biodiversity loss.

Codes

(a) Only I
(b) Only II
(c) Both I and II
(d) None of the above

28. Consider the following statements and choose the correct option.

I. Scavengers are animals that feed on dead and decaying plants and animals.

II. A mangrove is a shrub or small tree that grows in coastal saline or brackish water.

Codes

(a) Only I (b) Only II
(c) Both I and II (d) Neither I nor II

Darken your choice with HB Pencil

1.	ⓐ ⓑ ⓒ ⓓ	6.	ⓐ ⓑ ⓒ ⓓ	11.	ⓐ ⓑ ⓒ ⓓ	16.	ⓐ ⓑ ⓒ ⓓ	21.	ⓐ ⓑ ⓒ ⓓ	26.	ⓐ ⓑ ⓒ ⓓ
2.	ⓐ ⓑ ⓒ ⓓ	7.	ⓐ ⓑ ⓒ ⓓ	12.	ⓐ ⓑ ⓒ ⓓ	17.	ⓐ ⓑ ⓒ ⓓ	22.	ⓐ ⓑ ⓒ ⓓ	27.	ⓐ ⓑ ⓒ ⓓ
3.	ⓐ ⓑ ⓒ ⓓ	8.	ⓐ ⓑ ⓒ ⓓ	13.	ⓐ ⓑ ⓒ ⓓ	18.	ⓐ ⓑ ⓒ ⓓ	23.	ⓐ ⓑ ⓒ ⓓ	28.	ⓐ ⓑ ⓒ ⓓ
4.	ⓐ ⓑ ⓒ ⓓ	9.	ⓐ ⓑ ⓒ ⓓ	14.	ⓐ ⓑ ⓒ ⓓ	19.	ⓐ ⓑ ⓒ ⓓ	24.	ⓐ ⓑ ⓒ ⓓ		
5.	ⓐ ⓑ ⓒ ⓓ	10.	ⓐ ⓑ ⓒ ⓓ	15.	ⓐ ⓑ ⓒ ⓓ	20.	ⓐ ⓑ ⓒ ⓓ	25.	ⓐ ⓑ ⓒ ⓓ		

Chapter 11

Constitution of India

MCQs 1 Mark Questions

1. What is the significance of the Preamble in the Indian Constitution?
   (a) It states the objectives of the President.
   (b) It states the objectives of the election.
   (c) It states the objectives of the Constitution.
   (d) None of the above

2. Which among the following defines the set of rules to govern country?
   (a) Preamble (b) Sovereignty
   (c) Constitution (d) None of these

3. What do you mean by republican form of government?
   (a) No king in republic
   (b) No British in republic
   (c) No female in republic
   (d) None of the above

4. What is the meaning of the term sovereignty?
   (a) Freedom to establish new country
   (b) Freedom to govern oneself
   (c) People's government
   (d) None of the above

5. When did our Constitution came into force?
   (a) 26th January, 1950
   (b) 15th August, 1947
   (c) 2nd October, 1950
   (d) 26th November, 1949

6. On which date did the Constituent Assembly meet for the first time?
   (a) 9th August, 1942
   (b) 15th August, 1942
   (c) 9th December, 1946
   (d) 26th January, 1950

7. What do you mean by secular state?
   (a) States that don't have any official religion
   (b) States that don't have any king
   (c) States that don't have any Preamble
   (d) None of the above

8. The Constituent Assembly that drafted our Constitution was elected on the recommendation of ....
   (a) the Cripps Proposals
   (b) the Cabinet Mission
   (c) the Indian Independence Act
   (d) the Wavell Plan

9. Which of the following served as the background for the Indian Constitution?
   (a) The Government of India Act, 1935
   (b) Constitution of USA
   (c) Proposals of Cabinet Mission in 1946
   (d) Bill of Indian Independence of 1947

10. Who among the following was first President of the Constituent Assembly?
(a) Dr BR Ambedkar
(b) Dr Rajendra Prasad
(c) Shri KM Munshi
(d) Dr Sachchidananda Sinha

11. The members of the Constituent Assembly were elected by ....
(a) Provincial Assemblies
(b) representatives of the Princely States
(c) people
(d) the government

12. Complete the given analogy about the feature adopted in the Indian Constitution from other countries.
UK : Bicameralism : : USA : ?
(a) Fundamental Rights
(b) Justice
(c) Directive Principles of State Policy
(d) Republic

13. In 1934, ... demanded for a Constituent Assembly for the first time.
(a) Indian National Congress
(b) Swaraj Party
(c) Forward Block
(d) Communist Party

14. In which year, Constitution of India was amended for the first time?
(a) 1950 (b) 1951 (c) 1952 (d) 1953

15. Which among the following is the three tier of the government?
(a) Panchayati Raj
(b) State Government
(c) Municipal Corporation
(d) Union Territories

16. Which of the following is called 'Mini Constitution'?
(a) Government of India Act, 1935
(b) 42nd Constitutional Amendment
(c) 44th Constitutional Amendment
(d) Government of India Act, 1919

17. The idea of 'Concurrent List' in the Indian Constitution is taken from the Constitution of which country?
(a) Ireland (b) Canada
(c) Australia (d) Japan

18. What is not taken from British Constitution in the Constitution of India?
(a) Parliamentary rule
(b) Single citizenship
(c) Fundamental Rights
(d) Cabinet system

19. KM Munshi was related to which committee?
(a) Constitution Drafting Committee
(b) Preamble Committee
(c) Public Accounts Committee
(d) None of the above

20. The idea of a Constituent Assembly was put forward for the first time by ....
(a) MN Roy
(b) Dr BR Ambedkar
(c) Dr Rajendra Prasad
(d) Sardar Vallabhbhai Patel

21. Which among the following is not an organ of government in our country?
(a) Legislature
(b) Armed Forces
(c) Executive
(d) Judiciary

22. Who among the following was the Constitutional Advisor of the Constituent Assembly?
(a) Dr BR Ambedkar
(b) KM Munshi
(c) Sir BN Rau
(d) Jawaharlal Nehru

23. Who was the Chairman of the Drafting Committee of the Constitution?

(a) Jawaharlal Nehru
(b) Dr BR Ambedkar
(c) Subhash Chandra Bose
(d) Dr Rajendra Prasad

24. Identify the incorrectly matched pair.

(a) Part I – Union and its Territories
(b) Part II – Citizenship
(c) Part III – Directive Principles of State Policy
(d) Part VI – State Government

MCQs 2 Marks Questions

25. Match the following.

	List I (Constitutional Features)		List II (Sources)
A.	Rule of Law	1.	German Constitution
B.	Directive Principles	2.	USSR Constitution
C.	Fundamental Duties	3.	Irish Constitution
D.	Suspension of Fundamental Rights during Emergency	4.	British Constitution

Codes

	A	B	C	D		A	B	C	D
(a)	4	2	1	3	(b)	4	3	2	1
(c)	2	3	4	1	(d)	2	1	4	3

26. Consider the following statements and choose the correct option.

I. The original Constitution had 10 schedules.
II. The political part of the Indian Constitution is taken from the British Constitution.
III. Article 368 is related to the Constitutional Amendment.

Codes

(a) I and II (b) Only I
(c) Only III (d) I, II and III

27. Identify the feature of the government with the help of the information given below.

- It refers to the existence of more than one level of government in the country.
- Panchayati Raj is one of the components of such feature.

(a) Bicameralism
(b) Federalism
(c) Republic
(d) Single citizenship

28. Read the following statements and identifies which ones are true (T) and which ones are false (F).

I. Constitution tells us about the fundamental nature of our society.
II. Constitution defines a country's political system.
III. Constitution ensures the protection of minorities through rules and regulations.

Codes

	I	II	III		I	II	III
(a)	T	T	T	(b)	F	T	F
(c)	T	F	T	(d)	F	F	F

Darken your choice with HB Pencil

1. ⓐ ⓑ ⓒ ⓓ	6. ⓐ ⓑ ⓒ ⓓ	11. ⓐ ⓑ ⓒ ⓓ	16. ⓐ ⓑ ⓒ ⓓ	21. ⓐ ⓑ ⓒ ⓓ	26. ⓐ ⓑ ⓒ ⓓ
2. ⓐ ⓑ ⓒ ⓓ	7. ⓐ ⓑ ⓒ ⓓ	12. ⓐ ⓑ ⓒ ⓓ	17. ⓐ ⓑ ⓒ ⓓ	22. ⓐ ⓑ ⓒ ⓓ	27. ⓐ ⓑ ⓒ ⓓ
3. ⓐ ⓑ ⓒ ⓓ	8. ⓐ ⓑ ⓒ ⓓ	13. ⓐ ⓑ ⓒ ⓓ	18. ⓐ ⓑ ⓒ ⓓ	23. ⓐ ⓑ ⓒ ⓓ	28. ⓐ ⓑ ⓒ ⓓ
4. ⓐ ⓑ ⓒ ⓓ	9. ⓐ ⓑ ⓒ ⓓ	14. ⓐ ⓑ ⓒ ⓓ	19. ⓐ ⓑ ⓒ ⓓ	24. ⓐ ⓑ ⓒ ⓓ	
5. ⓐ ⓑ ⓒ ⓓ	10. ⓐ ⓑ ⓒ ⓓ	15. ⓐ ⓑ ⓒ ⓓ	20. ⓐ ⓑ ⓒ ⓓ	25. ⓐ ⓑ ⓒ ⓓ	

Chapter 12

Parliament

MCQs 1 Mark Questions

1. What is the minimum age for holding office in the Lok Sabha?
(a) 18 years (b) 21 years
(c) 25 years (d) 30 years

2. What should be the interval between the two consecutive sessions of Parliament?
(a) Four months
(b) Six months
(c) 1 year
(d) Fixed by the President

3. Who presides over the joint session of both the Houses of the Parliament?
(a) Speaker (b) Vice-President
(c) President (d) Prime Minister

4. How many members in the Rajya Sabha are elected from the States and Union Territories?
(a) 245 (b) 238
(c) 250 (d) 252

5. What could be the maximum time limit of 'zero hour' in the Lok Sabha?
(a) 30 minutes
(b) One hour
(c) Indefinite period
(d) Two hours

6. Which type of election system is adopted in the election of the Lok Sabha?
(a) Regional Representation System
(b) Proportional Representation System
(c) Both (a) and (b)
(d) None of the above

7. For which of the following 'single transferable voting system' adopted in India?
(a) Rajya Sabha
(b) President
(c) State Legislative Council
(d) All of the above

8. The budget is also known as ....
(a) Annual Financial Statement
(b) Monthly Financial Statement
(c) Receipt and Expenditure Statement
(d) Taxation Statement

9. Who among the following decides whether a bill is a Money Bill or not?
(a) President
(b) Prime Minister
(c) Speaker of the Lok Sabha
(d) Finance Minister

10. Which among the following articles defines the Money Bill?
(a) Article 110 (b) Article 111
(c) Article 112 (d) Article 113

11. Who is the ex-officio Chairman of the Rajya Sabha?
(a) Prime Minister (b) President
(c) Vice-President (d) Senate

12. Complete the given analogy.
Lok Sabha : 552 members : : Rajya Sabha : ?
(a) 250 (b) 245
(c) 266 (d) 230

13. .... is not subject to dissolution by the President.
(a) Lok Sabha
(b) Rajya Sabha
(c) Both (a) and (b)
(d) None of the above

14. Who needs to sign the bill passed by the Parliament for becoming a law?
(a) President
(b) Prime Minister
(c) Finance Minister
(d) Chief Justice of India

15. The sessions of each House of the Parliament is summoned by the ....
(a) Lok Sabha
(b) Speaker
(c) Deputy Speaker
(d) President

16. How are the members of the Rajya Sabha elected?
(a) By the Lok Sabha Speaker in consultation with the President.
(b) Nominated by the President in consultation with the Council of Ministers.
(c) Directly by the people.
(d) By the members of the State Legislative Assembly of each state.

17. A motion of no confidence against the government can be introduced in ....
(a) Rajya Sabha (b) Lok Sabha
(c) Both (a) and (b) (d) None of these

18. Which of the following is not the session of the Lok Sabha?
(a) Budget Session
(b) Monsoon Session
(c) Summer Session
(d) Winter Session

19. Name the only Lok Sabha Speaker who became the President of India.
(a) VV Giri
(b) Zail Singh
(c) Neelam Sanjiva Reddy
(d) S Radhakrishnan

20. The Speaker of the Lok Sabha addresses his letter of resignation to the ....
(a) Prime Minister of India
(b) President of India
(c) Deputy Speaker of Lok Sabha
(d) Vice-President of India

21. In which House of the Parliament, the presiding officer is not a member of the house?
(a) Lok Sabha
(b) Rajya Sabha
(c) Vidhan Sabha
(d) Vidhan Parishad

22. What is the term of member of the Rajya Sabha?
(a) 3 years (b) 4 years
(c) 5 years (d) 6 years

23. How many members are nominated by the President in the Rajya Sabha?
(a) 2 (b) 10
(c) 12 (d) 15

24.

The person in the above image is known as the Father of Lok Sabha. Identify him.

(a) GV Mavalankar
(b) Rabi Ray
(c) PA Sangma
(d) Balram Jakhar

25. Who among the following is the presiding officer of the Lok Sabha?

(a) President
(b) Vice-President
(c) Speaker of Lok Sabha
(d) Prime Minister

26. Which of the following is the supreme law making institution in India?

(a) Supreme Court
(b) Rajya Sabha
(c) Lok Sabha
(d) Parliament

27. Identify the Union territories that has/have elected members in Rajya Sabha.

(a) Delhi
(b) Puducherry
(c) Ladakh
(d) Both (a) and (b)

MCQs 2 Marks Questions

28. Which of the following is/are related to the Constitution of India?

I. Preamble of the Indian Constitution is known as the soul of the Constitution.

II. Part-IV of the Indian Constitution deals with the DPSPs.

Codes

(a) Neither I nor II (b) Both I and II
(c) Only I (d) Only II

29. There are two statements marked as Assertion (A) and Reason (R). Mark your answer as per the codes given below.

Assertion (A) Under Article 368, the Parliament can amend any part of the Constitution.

Reason (R) The Parliament is the Supreme Legislative body elected by the people of India.

Codes

(a) Both A and R are true and R is the correct explanation of A
(b) Both A and R are true, but R is not the correct explanation of A
(c) A is true, but R is false
(d) A is false, but R is true

30. Identify the incorrectly matched pair.

I. Parliament	– Legislative bodies of Central Government
II. Lok Sabha	– Lower House
III. Rajya Sabha	– Upper House
IV. House of Commons	– Upper House

Codes

(a) Only I (b) Only II
(c) III and IV (d) Only IV

31. Read the following statements and select the correct option.

I. Coalition Governments are formed when a single party doesn't get majority positions in Lok Sabha.

II. The leader of the majority party becomes the Prime Minister of the country.

III. Rajya Sabha is the permanent house of the Parliament.

IV. A bill can only become a law after it has been passed by both houses.

Codes

(a) I and II

(b) II, III and IV

(c) I, III and IV

(d) All of the above

32. There are two statements marked as Assertion (A) and Reason (R). Mark your answer as per the codes given below.

Assertion (A) The opposition party holds an equal position as the majority party.

Reason (R) The opposition in Parliament is formed by all the political parties that oppose the majority party/coalition formed.

Codes

(a) Both A and R are true and R is the correct explanation of A

(b) Both A and R are true, but R is not the correct explanation of A

(c) A is true, but R is false

(d) A is false, but R is true

Darken your choice with HB Pencil

1.	ⓐ ⓑ ⓒ ⓓ	7.	ⓐ ⓑ ⓒ ⓓ	13.	ⓐ ⓑ ⓒ ⓓ	19.	ⓐ ⓑ ⓒ ⓓ	25.	ⓐ ⓑ ⓒ ⓓ	31.	ⓐ ⓑ ⓒ ⓓ
2.	ⓐ ⓑ ⓒ ⓓ	8.	ⓐ ⓑ ⓒ ⓓ	14.	ⓐ ⓑ ⓒ ⓓ	20.	ⓐ ⓑ ⓒ ⓓ	26.	ⓐ ⓑ ⓒ ⓓ	32.	ⓐ ⓑ ⓒ ⓓ
3.	ⓐ ⓑ ⓒ ⓓ	9.	ⓐ ⓑ ⓒ ⓓ	15.	ⓐ ⓑ ⓒ ⓓ	21.	ⓐ ⓑ ⓒ ⓓ	27.	ⓐ ⓑ ⓒ ⓓ		
4.	ⓐ ⓑ ⓒ ⓓ	10.	ⓐ ⓑ ⓒ ⓓ	16.	ⓐ ⓑ ⓒ ⓓ	22.	ⓐ ⓑ ⓒ ⓓ	28.	ⓐ ⓑ ⓒ ⓓ		
5.	ⓐ ⓑ ⓒ ⓓ	11.	ⓐ ⓑ ⓒ ⓓ	17.	ⓐ ⓑ ⓒ ⓓ	23.	ⓐ ⓑ ⓒ ⓓ	29.	ⓐ ⓑ ⓒ ⓓ		
6.	ⓐ ⓑ ⓒ ⓓ	12.	ⓐ ⓑ ⓒ ⓓ	18.	ⓐ ⓑ ⓒ ⓓ	24.	ⓐ ⓑ ⓒ ⓓ	30.	ⓐ ⓑ ⓒ ⓓ		

Chapter 13

Judiciary

MCQs 1 Mark Questions

1. How many levels of court are there in India?

(a) Multiple (b) One

(c) Two (d) None of these

2. Judiciary system provide mechanism for resolving disputes between ....

(a) citizens

(b) two state government

(c) citizens and government

(d) All of the above

3. Which state shares the same High Court?

(a) Punjab and Haryana

(b) Arunachal Pradesh and Mizoram

(c) Both (a) and (b)

(d) None of the above

4. How many High Courts are there in India?

(a) 25 (b) 26

(c) 27 (d) 24

5. The High Court of Delhi came into existence in ....

(a) 1860 (b) 1972

(c) 1966 (d) 1862

6. High Courts were first established in which of the three presidency cities?

(a) Calcutta, Bombay, Madras

(b) Madras, Tamil Nadu, Punjab

(c) J and K, UP, Haryana

(d) Punjab, Chandigarh, Madras

7. In which year, High Courts was first established?

(a) 1860 (b) 1980

(c) 1972 (d) 1862

8. The Supreme Court was established in the year ....

(a) 1950 (b) 1949 (c) 1962 (d) 1980

9. At what age, judge of the High Court gets retired from his/her post?

(a) 62 years (b) 65 years

(c) 60 years (d) 64 years

10. What is the full form of PIL?

(a) Public Interest Limited

(b) Public Interference Limited

(c) Public Interest Litigation

(d) None of the above

11. Identify the only Union Territory which has a High Court of its own.

(a) Puducherry

(b) Delhi

(c) Chandigarh

(d) Daman and Diu

12. Who among the following was first woman judge of India?
(a) Leila Seth (b) Anna Chandy
(c) Fathima Beevi (d) Sujata Manohar

13. Which among the following is the correct age of retirement of judge of Supreme Court?
(a) 58 years (b) 60 years
(c) 62 years (d) 65 years

14. Which of the following High Courts has jurisdiction over more than one State/ Union Territories ?
(a) Mumbai (b) Guwahati
(c) Kolkata (d) All of these

15. Who among the following decides the number of judges in a High Court ?
(a) The President
(b) Chief Minister of the state
(c) Prime Minister
(d) Parliament

16. The Chief Justice and other judges of the High Court are appointed by the ....
(a) President
(b) Chief Justice of the Supreme Court
(c) Governor of the concerned state
(d) Attorney General of India

17. The oath to a High Court judge is administered by which of the following?
(a) Chief Justice of India
(b) Chief Justice of High Court
(c) President
(d) Governor of the concerned state

18. In India, the power to increase the number of judges in the Supreme Court lies with ....
(a) the President of India
(b) the Chief Justice of India
(c) the Union Ministry of Law
(d) the Parliament of India

19. Disputes between states of India comes to the Supreme Court under which jurisdiction?
(a) Original jurisdiction
(b) Appellate jurisdiction
(c) Advisory jurisdiction
(d) None of the above

20. Under the Constitution, the power to issue a writ of Habeas Corpus is vested in.......... .
(a) High Court
(b) Supreme Court
(c) Both Supreme Court and High Court
(d) All courts down to the District Courts

21. Who among the following appoints the district judges in the state?
(a) President of India
(b) Chief Justice of the High Court
(c) Governor of the state
(d) Parliament

22. District courts are also known as ....
(a) Lower courts (b) Apex courts
(c) Sessions courts (d) Both (a) and (c)

23. During the British period, the High Court was not established in which of the following regions?
(a) Bombay (b) Madras
(c) Calcutta (d) Punjab

MCQs 2 Marks Questions

24. Consider the following statements regarding Supreme Court which is a court of record.
I. It can punish for it's contempt.
II. It's decisions are admitted as evidence and cannot be questioned by any court.
III. It has to keep a record of all the important cases in India.

IV. It's decisions once taken are binding upon it.

Which of the following statements are correct?

(a) I, II and III
(b) I and II
(c) I, III and IV
(d) I, II, III and IV

25. There are two statements marked as Assertion (A) and Reason (R). Mark your answer as per the codes given below.

Assertion (A) A Supreme Court judge is appointed by the President.

Reason (R) There should be minimum interference of the Executive body.

Codes

(a) Both A and R are true and R is the correct explanation of A
(b) Both A and R are true, but R is not the correct explanation of A
(c) A is true, but R is false
(d) A is false, but R is true

26. Identify the incorrectly matched pair.

Organ		Function
I. Judiciary	–	Settles disputes
II. Permanent Executive	–	Administers laws
III. Political Executive	–	Creates laws
IV. Legislature	–	Executes laws

Codes

(a) Only I (b) II and III
(c) III and IV (d) Only IV

27. Read the following statements and choose the correct option.

I. The Governor appoints the Chief Minister of a state.
II. The Chief Minister is an elected head of the state.
III. The Governor of a state is appointed by the Prime Minister.

Codes

(a) Only I (b) I and II
(c) II and III (d) I, II and III

Darken your choice with HB Pencil

1.	ⓐ ⓑ ⓒ ⓓ	6.	ⓐ ⓑ ⓒ ⓓ	11.	ⓐ ⓑ ⓒ ⓓ	16.	ⓐ ⓑ ⓒ ⓓ	21.	ⓐ ⓑ ⓒ ⓓ	26.	ⓐ ⓑ ⓒ ⓓ
2.	ⓐ ⓑ ⓒ ⓓ	7.	ⓐ ⓑ ⓒ ⓓ	12.	ⓐ ⓑ ⓒ ⓓ	17.	ⓐ ⓑ ⓒ ⓓ	22.	ⓐ ⓑ ⓒ ⓓ	27.	ⓐ ⓑ ⓒ ⓓ
3.	ⓐ ⓑ ⓒ ⓓ	8.	ⓐ ⓑ ⓒ ⓓ	13.	ⓐ ⓑ ⓒ ⓓ	18.	ⓐ ⓑ ⓒ ⓓ	23.	ⓐ ⓑ ⓒ ⓓ		
4.	ⓐ ⓑ ⓒ ⓓ	9.	ⓐ ⓑ ⓒ ⓓ	14.	ⓐ ⓑ ⓒ ⓓ	19.	ⓐ ⓑ ⓒ ⓓ	24.	ⓐ ⓑ ⓒ ⓓ		
5.	ⓐ ⓑ ⓒ ⓓ	10.	ⓐ ⓑ ⓒ ⓓ	15.	ⓐ ⓑ ⓒ ⓓ	20.	ⓐ ⓑ ⓒ ⓓ	25.	ⓐ ⓑ ⓒ ⓓ		

Chapter 14

General Awareness

(Books & Authors, Awards & Honours, Capital & Currencies, International Organisations, Research Institutes, Miscellaneous)

MCQs 1 Mark Questions

1. Who among the following wrote the book 'India Wins Freedom'?
   (a) Akhilesh Tilotia
   (b) Amitav Ghosh
   (c) Abul Kalam Azad
   (d) Atal Bihari Vajpayee

2. Which of the following is not written by Munshi Premchand?
   (a) Gaban (b) Godan
   (c) Gillu (d) Mansarovar

3. Which of the following books have been written by Abu'l Fazl?
   (a) Ain-i-Akbari (b) Akbarnama
   (c) Both (a) and (b) (d) Kafan

4. The 'Arthashastra' is a treatise book on which one of the following?
   (a) Religion in Administration
   (b) Political Philosophy
   (c) Environmental
   (d) Economics

5. For which of the following fields is/are Nobel Prize awarded?
   (a) Literature, Peace and Economics
   (b) Physics and Chemistry
   (c) Physiology and Medicine
   (d) All of the above

6. The first Indian to receive Nobel Prize in Literature was ....
   (a) Mother Teresa
   (b) CV Raman
   (c) Rabindranath Tagore
   (d) Sarojini Naidu

7. .... is the capital of Russia.
   (a) Moscow (b) New Delhi
   (c) Havana (d) Prague

8. Identify the capital city of Italy which is also referred to as the 'Eternal City' of the world.
   (a) Rome
   (b) Washington DC
   (c) Tripoli
   (d) Skopje

9. What is the capital city of the Philippines?

(a) Warsaw (b) Quezon City
(c) Manila (d) Davao City

10. What is the capital city of Cambodia?

(a) Phnom Penh (b) Hanoi
(c) Lamur (d) Bangkok

11. Identify the national currency of Ethiopia.

(a) Ethiopian Guilder (b) Ethiopian Euros
(c) Ethiopian Dollar (d) Ethiopian Birr

12. Complete the given analogy.

Germany : Euro :: Myanmar : ?

(a) Dollar (b) Kyat
(c) Dinar (d) Pound

13. Which among the following two countries use Euro as their currency?

(a) India and Nepal
(b) Pakistan and India
(c) Germany and France
(d) Russia and China

14. Which among the following is the currency of China?

(a) Ruble (b) Yuan
(c) Euro (d) Pound

15. Which of the following is/are not associated with the UNO?

(a) ILO (b) WHO
(c) ASEAN (d) All of these

16. Which of the following is not a chief organ of the United Nations Organisation?

(a) International Labour Organisation
(b) Security Council
(c) International Court of Justice
(d) General Assembly

17. What is the full form of ESCAP?

(a) European Society Council for Africa and Pacific
(b) Economic and Social Commission for Asia and Pacific
(c) Economic and Social Commission for Africa and Pacific
(d) None of the above

18. The Secretary-General of UNO is appointed by ………… .

(a) the General Assembly
(b) the Security Council
(c) the International Court of Justice
(d) the General Assembly on the recommendations of the Security Council

19. Identify the correctly matched pair.

	UN Organisations		**Headquarters**
(a)	UNESCO	–	Geneva
(b)	IMF	–	Paris
(c)	ILO	–	Washington
(d)	UNIDO	–	Vienna

20. Identify the organisation associated with the emblem shown in the picture given below.

(a) WHO (b) ASEAN
(c) UN (d) WTO

21. Indian Institute of Remote Sensing is located in which city?

(a) Dehradun (b) Shimla
(c) Kullu (d) Bilaspur

22. Central Rice Research Institute is located in which city?

(a) Shimla (b) Chennai
(c) Cuttack (d) Chandigarh

23. Identify the incorrectly matched pair.
(a) ASEAN - Jakarta
(b) Interpol - Lyon
(c) SAARC - New Delhi
(d) International Committee of the Red Cross – Geneva

24. Where in India 'National Institute of Agricultural Marketing' located?
(a) Ludhiana (b) Nagpur
(c) Indore (d) Jaipur

25. National Dairy Research Institute is located in ....
(a) Kerala (b) Udaipur
(c) Karnal (d) Rohtak

26. National Institute of Nutrition is situated in ....
(a) Aurangabad
(b) Hyderabad
(c) Mizoram
(d) Bengaluru

27. Which country is known as Land of Rising Sun?
(a) Japan
(b) China
(c) India
(d) USA

28. Which bank is known as the bankers bank of India?
(a) SBI
(b) Reserve Bank of India
(c) Bank of Baroda
(d) Punjab National Bank

29. Which state has the longest coastline in India?
(a) Gujarat
(b) Odisha
(c) Assam
(d) Karnataka

MCQs 2 Marks Questions

30. Which among the following is/are the aim(s) of the United Nations?
I. Providing full employment
II. Providing conditions of economic growth

Codes
(a) Only I (b) Only II
(c) Both I and II (d) None of these

31. There are two statements marked as Assertion (A) and Reason (R). Mark your answer as per the codes given below.

Assertion (A) The General Assembly is one of the principal organ of the United Nations which consists of all the members of United Nations.

Reason (R) The Resolutions or Declaration of the General Assembly are not binding upon the states. They are merely recommendations.

Codes
(a) Both A and R are true and R is the correct explanation of A
(b) Both A and R are true, but R is not the correct explanation of A
(c) A is true, but R is false
(d) A is false, but R is true

32. Match the following

List I (Books)	List II (Authors)
A. Gitanjali	1. RK Narayan
B. Malgudi Days	2. Rabindranath Tagore
C. Discovery of India	3. MK Gandhi
D. My Experiments with Truth	4. Jawaharlal Nehru

Codes

	A	B	C	D		A	B	C	D
(a)	1	2	3	4	(b)	2	1	4	3
(c)	3	2	4	1	(d)	4	3	1	2

33. Match the following

List I (International Organisation)	List II (Headquarters)
A. UNO	1. Geneva, Switzerland
B. IMF	2. Washington DC
C. WTO	3. New York
D. UNESCO	4. Paris

Codes

	A	B	C	D		A	B	C	D
(a)	3	2	1	4	(b)	1	2	3	4
(c)	2	1	3	4	(d)	4	2	1	3

34. Consider the following statements and choose the correct option.

I. Nepal is the only nation that does not have a rectangular flag.

II. Pound is the currency of England.

III. Colombo is the capital city of Sri Lanka.

Codes

(a) Only I (b) I and II

(c) Only III (d) I, II and III

35. Which of the following novels are written by Munshi Premchand?

I. Gaban

II. Godan

III. Nirmala

IV. Gunaho ka devta

Choose the correct option.

(a) II and III

(b) II, III and IV

(c) I, II and III

(d) I, II and IV

36. Which of the following full forms are correct?

I. GDP – Gross Development Product

II. ATM – Automated Teller Machine

III. AIDS – Acquired Immuno Deficiency Syndrome

Codes

(a) II and III

(b) I, II and III

(c) I and III

(d) II and I

Darken your choice with HB Pencil

1. ⓐ ⓑ ⓒ ⓓ	7. ⓐ ⓑ ⓒ ⓓ	13. ⓐ ⓑ ⓒ ⓓ	19. ⓐ ⓑ ⓒ ⓓ	25. ⓐ ⓑ ⓒ ⓓ	31. ⓐ ⓑ ⓒ ⓓ
2. ⓐ ⓑ ⓒ ⓓ	8. ⓐ ⓑ ⓒ ⓓ	14. ⓐ ⓑ ⓒ ⓓ	20. ⓐ ⓑ ⓒ ⓓ	26. ⓐ ⓑ ⓒ ⓓ	32. ⓐ ⓑ ⓒ ⓓ
3. ⓐ ⓑ ⓒ ⓓ	9. ⓐ ⓑ ⓒ ⓓ	15. ⓐ ⓑ ⓒ ⓓ	21. ⓐ ⓑ ⓒ ⓓ	27. ⓐ ⓑ ⓒ ⓓ	33. ⓐ ⓑ ⓒ ⓓ
4. ⓐ ⓑ ⓒ ⓓ	10. ⓐ ⓑ ⓒ ⓓ	16. ⓐ ⓑ ⓒ ⓓ	22. ⓐ ⓑ ⓒ ⓓ	28. ⓐ ⓑ ⓒ ⓓ	34. ⓐ ⓑ ⓒ ⓓ
5. ⓐ ⓑ ⓒ ⓓ	11. ⓐ ⓑ ⓒ ⓓ	17. ⓐ ⓑ ⓒ ⓓ	23. ⓐ ⓑ ⓒ ⓓ	29. ⓐ ⓑ ⓒ ⓓ	35. ⓐ ⓑ ⓒ ⓓ
6. ⓐ ⓑ ⓒ ⓓ	12. ⓐ ⓑ ⓒ ⓓ	18. ⓐ ⓑ ⓒ ⓓ	24. ⓐ ⓑ ⓒ ⓓ	30. ⓐ ⓑ ⓒ ⓓ	36. ⓐ ⓑ ⓒ ⓓ

Chapter 15

Science and Technology

MCQs 1 Mark Questions

1. Which one of the following is an 'Air-to-Air' missile?
(a) Astra (b) Akash
(c) Becquerel (d) Prithvi

2. What was the name of the space shuttle that landed man on the Moon?
(a) Apollo (b) Challenger
(c) Columbia (d) Eagle

3. An astronaut in outer space will observe sky as ....
(a) black (b) white
(c) rich blue (d) light blue

4. Where is the headquarters of the Indian Institute of Astrophysics (IIA) located?
(a) New Delhi
(b) Bengaluru
(c) Guwahati
(d) Kochi

5. Vikram Sarabhai Space Centre (VSSC) is located at ....
(a) Mumbai
(b) Bengaluru
(c) Hyderabad
(d) Thiruvananthapuram

6. What is the name of the Light Combat Aircraft developed by Indian indigenously?
(a) Tejas (b) BrahMos
(c) Chetak (d) Astra

7. Which one of the following institutes is wrongly matched with its location?
(a) Central Building Research Institute – Roorkee
(b) Central Arid Zone Research Institute – Jodhpur
(c) Central Drug Research Institute – Kanpur
(d) Central Institute of Mining and Fuel Research – Dhanbad

8. INS 'Virat' serves the Indian Navy. Identify it's type.
(a) Freighter (b) Submarine
(c) Aircraft carrier (d) Gunboat

9. Which one of the following refers to the first nuclear reactor of India?
(a) Kamini (b) Apsara
(c) Urvashi (d) Rohini

10. When did the first Indian Satellite Aryabhatta was launched?
(a) 1974 (b) 1975
(c) 1976 (d) 1977

11. Nuclear explosive devices were tested in India at ....

(a) Bengaluru (b) Sriharikota
(c) Kanchipuram (d) Pokhran

12. Which city receives the highest cosmic radiation amongst the following?

(a) Delhi (b) Kolkata
(c) Mumbai (d) Chennai

13. The process in which nitrogen is released into the atmosphere is ....

(a) nitrification
(b) ammonification
(c) denitrification
(d) biological nitrogen fixation

14. Saha Institute of Nuclear Physics is situated at ....

(a) New Delhi (b) Mumbai
(c) Kolkata (d) Chennai

15. Who among the following was the first person to enter into space?

(a) Alan Shepard
(b) Yuri Gagarin
(c) Edward H White
(d) Valentina Tereshkova

16. Complete the given analogy.

Thermometer : Temperature :: Glucometer : ?

(a) Body sugar
(b) Body resistance
(c) Blood
(d) Blood sugar

17. What is the process called by which solid changes into gas without changing into liquid?

(a) Vapourisation
(b) Boiling
(c) Sublimation
(d) Condensation

18. The instrument in the given diagram is used to measure atmospheric pressure. Identify the instrument.

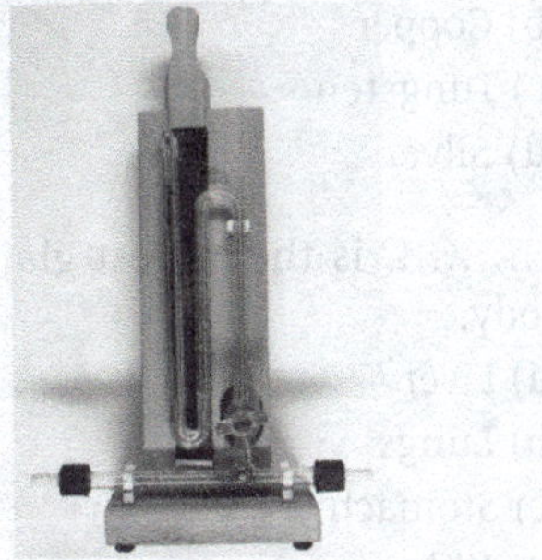

(a) Barometer
(b) Meter Gauge
(c) Anemometer
(d) Richter Scale

19. Richter Scale is used to measure which among the following?

(a) Volcanoes
(b) Wind speed
(c) Earthquake
(d) Humidity

20. Tarapur Nuclear Power Plant is located in which state?

(a) Andhra Pradesh
(b) Maharashtra
(c) Karnataka
(d) Odisha

21. Satish Dhawan Space Centre is located in which state?

(a) Karnataka (b) Andhra Pradesh
(c) Haryana (d) Odisha

22. Identify the incorrectly matched pair.

(a) Tesla – Electric Car
(b) Bitcoin – Cryptocurrency
(c) Pokemon Go – Augmented Reality Mobile Game
(d) Zoom – OTT Streaming Platform

23. Identify the only metal that is present in liquid form.
(a) Mercury
(b) Copper
(c) Tungsten
(d) Silver

24. ………… is the largest gland of human body.
(a) Liver
(b) Lungs
(c) Stomach
(d) Kidneys

25. Choose the incorrectly matched pair regarding quantities and its SI units.
(a) Mass - Kilogram
(b) Temperature - Kelvin
(c) Force - Ampere
(d) Volume - Cubic meter

MCQs 2 Marks Questions

26. There are two statements marked as Assertion (A) and Reason (R). Mark your answer as per the codes given below.

Assertion (A) When sugar pour in water, then taste of water become sweet.

Reason (R) Sugar will dissolve into the water and will create a solution.

Codes
(a) Both A and R are true and R is the correct explanation of A
(b) Both A and R are true, but R is not the correct explanation of A
(c) A is true, but R is false
(d) R is true, but A is false

27. Consider the following statements and choose the correct option.
I. Global Positioning System (GPS) was developed by the US military for the measurement of accurate position, movement and time.
II. The first GPS satellite was launched in 1978.

Codes
(a) Only I (b) Only II
(c) Both I and II (d) Neither I nor II

28. Consider the following statements and choose the correct option.
I. BrahMos is the first supersonic operational cruise missile in the world.
II. BrahMos can be launched from multiple platforms such as submarines, ships, aircraft and land based Mobile Autonomous Launchers (MAL).

Codes
(a) Only I
(b) Only II
(c) Both I and II
(d) Neither I nor II

29. Plastic bags are a potential hazard to the environment. Which of the following options correctly describes this?
(a) They are light in weight and hence cause nuisance by flying.
(b) Toxic chemicals are used in their production.
(c) They are non-resistant to heat.
(d) They are non-biodegradable.

30. Match the following.

List I (Organ)	**List II** (System)
A. Spinal Cord	1. Nervous system
B. Kidneys	2. Excretory system
C. Lungs	3. Respiratory system
D. Liver	4. Digestive system

Codes

	A	B	C	D		A	B	C	D
(a)	1	2	3	4	(b)	2	1	4	3
(c)	3	2	4	1	(d)	4	3	1	2

31. There are two statements marked as Assertion (A) and Reason (R). Mark your answer as per the codes given below.

Assertion (A) GPS was developed for military purpose.

Reason (R) GPS is used in tablets/laptops, computers, watches, mobile phones and cars.

Codes

(a) Both A and R are true and R is the correct explanation of A
(b) Both A and R are true, but R is not the correct explanation of A
(c) A is true, but R is false
(d) A is false, but R is true

32. Consider the following statements and choose the correct option.

I. Human heart is made up of four chambers.
II. Arteries are not a part of circulatory system.
III. Diabetes is caused due to deficiency of insulin.

Codes

(a) I and II (b) I and III
(c) I and II (d) I, II, III

33. Consider the following statements and choose the correct option.

I. Carbohydrates and fats are sources of energy.
II. Egg is an important source of protein
III. 60-75% of human body is made up of water.

Codes

(a) I and II
(b) II and III
(c) I and III
(d) I, II and III

Darken your choice with HB Pencil

1.	ⓐ ⓑ ⓒ ⓓ	7.	ⓐ ⓑ ⓒ ⓓ	13.	ⓐ ⓑ ⓒ ⓓ	19.	ⓐ ⓑ ⓒ ⓓ	25.	ⓐ ⓑ ⓒ ⓓ	31.	ⓐ ⓑ ⓒ ⓓ
2.	ⓐ ⓑ ⓒ ⓓ	8.	ⓐ ⓑ ⓒ ⓓ	14.	ⓐ ⓑ ⓒ ⓓ	20.	ⓐ ⓑ ⓒ ⓓ	26.	ⓐ ⓑ ⓒ ⓓ	32.	ⓐ ⓑ ⓒ ⓓ
3.	ⓐ ⓑ ⓒ ⓓ	9.	ⓐ ⓑ ⓒ ⓓ	15.	ⓐ ⓑ ⓒ ⓓ	21.	ⓐ ⓑ ⓒ ⓓ	27.	ⓐ ⓑ ⓒ ⓓ	33.	ⓐ ⓑ ⓒ ⓓ
4.	ⓐ ⓑ ⓒ ⓓ	10.	ⓐ ⓑ ⓒ ⓓ	16.	ⓐ ⓑ ⓒ ⓓ	22.	ⓐ ⓑ ⓒ ⓓ	28.	ⓐ ⓑ ⓒ ⓓ		
5.	ⓐ ⓑ ⓒ ⓓ	11.	ⓐ ⓑ ⓒ ⓓ	17.	ⓐ ⓑ ⓒ ⓓ	23.	ⓐ ⓑ ⓒ ⓓ	29.	ⓐ ⓑ ⓒ ⓓ		
6.	ⓐ ⓑ ⓒ ⓓ	12.	ⓐ ⓑ ⓒ ⓓ	18.	ⓐ ⓑ ⓒ ⓓ	24.	ⓐ ⓑ ⓒ ⓓ	30.	ⓐ ⓑ ⓒ ⓓ		

Chapter 16

Computer

MCQs 1 Mark Questions

1. Who among the following is the father of computer?
(a) James Gosling (b) Charles Babbage
(c) Dennis Ritchie (d) Bjarne Stroustrup

2. Identify the correct abbreviation of COMPUTER.
(a) Commonly Occupied Machines Used in Technical and Educational Research
(b) Commonly Operated Machines Used in Technical and Environmental Research
(c) Common Oriented Machines Used in Technical and Educational Research
(d) Common Operating Machines Used in Technical and Educational Research

3. Which of the following languages does the computer understand?
(a) Only C language
(b) Only Assembly language
(c) Only Binary language
(d) Only BASIC

4. Identify the brain of the computer from the options given below.
(a) Central Processing Unit
(b) Memory
(c) Arithmetic Logic Unit
(d) Control Unit

5. Which of the following units is responsible for converting the data received from the user into a computer understandable format?
(a) Output Unit
(b) Input Unit
(c) Memory Unit
(d) Arithmetic Logic Unit

6. Name the monitor which look like a television and are normally used with non-portable computer systems.
(a) LED
(b) LCD
(c) CRT
(d) Flat Panel Monitors

7. Which of the following parts of a processor contains the hardware necessary to perform all the operations required by a computer?
(a) Controller (b) Registers
(c) Cache (d) Data path

8. Which of the following is designed to control the operations of a computer?
(a) User
(b) Application software
(c) System software
(d) Utility software

9. Identify the device that devices use positional notation to represent a decimal number.
(a) Pascaline (b) Abacus
(c) Computer (d) Calculator

10. A light sensitive device that converts drawing, printed text or other images into digital form is known as ....
(a) keyboard (b) plotter
(c) scanner (d) OMR

11. Which protocol provides e-mail facility among different hosts?
(a) FTP (b) SMTP
(c) TELNET (d) SNMP

12. In how many generations, a computer can be classified?
(a) 3 (b) 4
(c) 5 (d) 6

13. Microprocessor was introduced in which generation of computer?
(a) Second Generation
(b) Fourth Generation
(c) Both (a) and (b)
(d) Third Generation

14. Identify the memory/memories that is/are non-volatile.
(a) SRAM (b) DRAM
(c) ROM (d) All of these

15. What is the term used for a temporary storage area that compensates for differences in data rate and data flow between devices?
(a) Buffer (b) Bus
(c) Channel (d) Modem

16. Identify the natural element which is the primary element in computer chips.
(a) Silicon (b) Carbon
(c) Iron (d) Uranium

17. Which of the following programs enable you to calculate numbers related to rows and columns?
(a) Window program
(b) Spreadsheet program
(c) Graphics program
(d) Word program

18. Which one of the following groups contains graphical file extensions?
(a) JPG, CPX, GCM
(b) GIF, TCE, WMF
(c) TCP, JPG, BMP
(d) JPG, GIF, BMP

19. What are five main components of a computer system?
(a) CPU, CD-ROM, Mouse, Keyboard, Sound card
(b) Memory, Video card, Monitor, Software, Hardware
(c) Modem, Keyboard, Word Processor, Printer, Screen
(d) CPU, Memory, System bus, Input, Output

20. Which of the following shortcut keys show the properties of a file?
(a) Alt + Ctrl
(b) Alt + P
(c) Alt + F3
(d) Alt + Enter

21. What is meant by DOM?
(a) Data Object Model
(b) Document Object Model
(c) Data Organisation Model
(d) Document Organisation Markup

22. Which of these form the basis of the IOS type of internet connection?
(a) Satellite
(b) Fiber optics
(c) Coaxial cables
(d) Bluetooth

23. Which type of wires are used for the fast speed internet connections?
(a) Co-axial cables
(b) Copper wires
(c) Optical fibre cables
(d) Hi tension wires

24. What is the full form of the abbreviation USB?
(a) Universal Serial Bus
(b) Uninterrupted System Boot
(c) Unified Serial Bus
(d) Universal System Business

25. What was the third generation of computers?
(a) Vacuum Tubes
(b) Integrated Circuits
(c) Transistors
(d) Microcomputers

MCQs 2 Marks Questions

26. Read the following statements and choose the correct option.
I. MS-Excel creates workbooks and each workbook may contain more work sheets.
II. A worksheet in MS-Excel 2000 package has a maximum of 256 columns and 65536 rows.
III. In Excel, columns are identified by a number and rows are identified by a letter.
IV. Cells are identified by the column letter and the row number in Excel.

Codes
(a) I, II and III
(b) II, III and IV
(c) I, III and IV
(d) I, II and IV

27. There are two statements marked as Assertion (A) and Reason (R). Mark your answer as per the codes given below.

Assertion (A) Operating system is a software program that enables the computer hardware to communicate and operate with the computer software.

Reason (R) Windows is an open source operating system.

Codes
(a) Both A and R are true and R is the correct explanation of A
(b) Both A and R are true, but R is not the correct explanation of A
(c) A is true, but R is false
(d) A is false, but R is true

28. There are two statements marked as Assertion(A) and Reason(R). Mark your answer as per the codes given below.

Assertion (A) The CPU performs the main function of information processing.

Reason (R) The ALU performs arithmetic and logical functions in the CPU.

Codes
(a) Both A and R are true and R is the correct explanation of A
(b) Both A and R are true, but R is not the correct explanation of A
(c) A is true, but R is false
(d) A is false, but R is true

29. Read the following statements and choose the correct option.

I. First computer that was made in India was Siddharth.

II. First computer in India was installed in main Post Office in Banglore.

Codes

(a) Only I

(b) Only II

(c) Both I and II

(d) None of the above

30. Match the following.

List I (Generation of Computer)	List II (Systems used in the machine)
A. First	1. Diodes and transistors
B. Second	2. Very Large Scale Integrated circuits
C. Fourth	3. Vacuum tubes

Codes

	A	B	C		A	B	C
(a)	3	1	2	(b)	1	2	3
(c)	3	2	1	(d)	2	3	1

Darken your choice with HB Pencil

1. ⓐ ⓑ ⓒ ⓓ	6. ⓐ ⓑ ⓒ ⓓ	11. ⓐ ⓑ ⓒ ⓓ	16. ⓐ ⓑ ⓒ ⓓ	21. ⓐ ⓑ ⓒ ⓓ	26. ⓐ ⓑ ⓒ ⓓ
2. ⓐ ⓑ ⓒ ⓓ	7. ⓐ ⓑ ⓒ ⓓ	12. ⓐ ⓑ ⓒ ⓓ	17. ⓐ ⓑ ⓒ ⓓ	22. ⓐ ⓑ ⓒ ⓓ	27. ⓐ ⓑ ⓒ ⓓ
3. ⓐ ⓑ ⓒ ⓓ	8. ⓐ ⓑ ⓒ ⓓ	13. ⓐ ⓑ ⓒ ⓓ	18. ⓐ ⓑ ⓒ ⓓ	23. ⓐ ⓑ ⓒ ⓓ	28. ⓐ ⓑ ⓒ ⓓ
4. ⓐ ⓑ ⓒ ⓓ	9. ⓐ ⓑ ⓒ ⓓ	14. ⓐ ⓑ ⓒ ⓓ	19. ⓐ ⓑ ⓒ ⓓ	24. ⓐ ⓑ ⓒ ⓓ	29. ⓐ ⓑ ⓒ ⓓ
5. ⓐ ⓑ ⓒ ⓓ	10. ⓐ ⓑ ⓒ ⓓ	15. ⓐ ⓑ ⓒ ⓓ	20. ⓐ ⓑ ⓒ ⓓ	25. ⓐ ⓑ ⓒ ⓓ	30. ⓐ ⓑ ⓒ ⓓ

Chapter 17

Defence

MCQs 1 Mark Questions

1. Where is the BARC's Research Centre located?
(a) Kolkata (b) Kashmir
(c) Gulmarg (d) All of these

2. The first nuclear reactor in India is ....
(a) Dhruva (b) Harsha
(c) Apsara (d) Vipula

3. Which atomic reactor is used for study of uranium heavy water lattice?
(a) Apsara (b) Zerlina
(c) Dhruva (d) Purnima I

4. The country's first indigenously built missile boat was ....
(a) INS Vibhuti (b) INS Vipul
(c) INS Savitri (d) INS Shakti

5. What is the range of missile 'Akash'?
(a) 4 km (b) 25 km
(c) 500 m to 9 km (d) 150 km

6. What was the code name of the operation to conduct nuclear test at Pokhran in May, 1998?
(a) Shakti (b) Hansa
(c) Buddha (d) Shiva

7. The range of missile Agni is approximately ....
(a) 150 km (b) 1200-2000 km
(c) 500 m to 9 km (d) 4 km

8. Which of the following is the first surface-to-surface missile in India?
(a) Prithvi (b) Trishul
(c) Agni (d) Nag

9. Which was the first tanker naval ship in India?
(a) INS Vinash (b) INS Khukri
(c) INS Shakti (d) INS Ajay

10. Which was the first frigate with modern guided missile in India?
(a) INS Shakti (b) INS Ajay
(c) INS Godavari (d) INS Sindhushastra

11. Who among the following is associated with first nuclear explosion in Pokhran?
(a) CNR Rao (b) Homi J Bhabha
(c) Anil Kakodkar (d) Raja Ramanna

12. Which among the following does not belong to the commissioned ranks in the army service?
(a) Brigadier (b) Colonel
(c) General (d) Commander

13. Name the first indigenous aircraft of India.
(a) HT-2 (b) Mikoyan MiG-25
(c) HF-25 MKI (d) Sukhoi Su-30 MKI

14. Which among the following is the first short-range surface-to-air missile in India?
(a) Akash (b) Trishul
(c) Nag (d) Prithvi

15. Name the first intermediate-range ballistic missile in India.
(a) Akash (b) Agni
(c) Prithvi (d) Trishul

16. Identify the first long-range multiple-target missile in India.
(a) Akash (b) Agni
(c) BrahMos (d) Prithvi

17. At which of the following places is the headquarters of South-Western Air Command located?
(a) Vadodara
(b) Jodhpur
(c) Pune
(d) Gandhinagar

18. National Defence Academy is situated in ....
(a) Kolkata (b) Mumbai
(c) Pune (d) Dehradun

19. LAC (Line of Actual Control) is an effective border between India and ....
(a) Pakistan (b) Bhutan
(c) Sri Lanka (d) China

20. Complete the given analogy.
Admiral : Navy : : ? : Indian Air Force
(a) Air Marshal
(b) Air Chief Marshal
(c) Air Vice-Marshal
(d) Flight Lieutenant

21. Identify the incorrectly matched pair.
(a) Air Force Academy – Hyderabad
(b) College of Military Engineering – Pune
(c) Institute of Armament Technology – Pune
(d) Naval College of Engineering – Kochi

22. Who among the following was the first Chief of Defence Staff of Indian Armed Forces?
(a) General Bipin Rawat
(b) General Anil Chauhan
(c) Lt. Manoj Pande
(d) Lt. BS Raju

23. Who was the first Commander in Chief of Indian Army?
(a) General Bipin Rawat
(b) KM Carlappa
(c) Sam Manekshaw
(d) Vikram Batra

24. In which year was the Kargil War fought?
(a) 1962 (b) 1971
(c) 1999 (d) 2005

25. The given picture is of Rafale Jet. These jets were procured from which country?

(a) France
(b) Germany
(c) USA
(d) Russia

MCQs 2 Marks Questions

26. Match the following.

List I (Name)	List II (Type of Army Weapon)
A. Swathi WLR	1. Aircraft Carrier
B. Prithvi-II	2. Missile
C. Vikrant	3. Radar

Codes

	A	B	C		A	B	C
(a)	1	3	2	(b)	1	2	3
(c)	3	2	1	(d)	3	1	2

27. Which of the following is/are the department(s) in Ministry of Defence?

I. Department of Defence

II. Department of Defence Research and Development

III. Department of Defence Production

IV. Department of Defence Finance

Codes

(a) I and II (b) I, II and III

(c) II, III and IV (d) Only I

28. Which of the following is/are Paramilitary Force(s) of India?

I. Indian Coast Guard

II. Assam Rifles

III. Directorate General of Resettlement

Codes

(a) I, II and III (b) I and III

(c) Only II (d) I and II

29. There are two statements marked as Assertion (A) and Reason(R). Mark your answer as per the codes given below.

Assertion (A) Admiral is the highest possible rank in Indian Army.

Reason (R) Chief of Staff of Indian Navy is known as General.

Codes

(a) Both A and R are true and R is the correct explanation of A

(b) Both A and R are true, but R is not the correct explanation of A

(c) A is true, but R is false

(d) A is false, but R is true

30. Consider the following statements and choose the correct option.

I. Prime Minister is the Supreme Commander of Armed Forces of India.

II. Responsibility of Defence of India rests with Union Cabinet.

III. Indian Army is ranked 4th largest army in the world.

Codes

(a) I and II (b) II and III

(c) I and III (d) I, II and III

31. Identify the personality with the help of the description given below.

- He was the chief of the army staff of the Indian Army during the Indo-Pakistani War of 1971.
- He was the first Indian Army officer to be promoted to the rank of field marshal.

(a) Sam Manekshaw (b) K M Cariappa

(c) Gopal Bewoor (d) Harbaksh Singh

Darken your choice with HB Pencil

1. ⓐ ⓑ ⓒ ⓓ	7. ⓐ ⓑ ⓒ ⓓ	13. ⓐ ⓑ ⓒ ⓓ	19. ⓐ ⓑ ⓒ ⓓ	25. ⓐ ⓑ ⓒ ⓓ	31. ⓐ ⓑ ⓒ ⓓ
2. ⓐ ⓑ ⓒ ⓓ	8. ⓐ ⓑ ⓒ ⓓ	14. ⓐ ⓑ ⓒ ⓓ	20. ⓐ ⓑ ⓒ ⓓ	26. ⓐ ⓑ ⓒ ⓓ	
3. ⓐ ⓑ ⓒ ⓓ	9. ⓐ ⓑ ⓒ ⓓ	15. ⓐ ⓑ ⓒ ⓓ	21. ⓐ ⓑ ⓒ ⓓ	27. ⓐ ⓑ ⓒ ⓓ	
4. ⓐ ⓑ ⓒ ⓓ	10. ⓐ ⓑ ⓒ ⓓ	16. ⓐ ⓑ ⓒ ⓓ	22. ⓐ ⓑ ⓒ ⓓ	28. ⓐ ⓑ ⓒ ⓓ	
5. ⓐ ⓑ ⓒ ⓓ	11. ⓐ ⓑ ⓒ ⓓ	17. ⓐ ⓑ ⓒ ⓓ	23. ⓐ ⓑ ⓒ ⓓ	29. ⓐ ⓑ ⓒ ⓓ	
6. ⓐ ⓑ ⓒ ⓓ	12. ⓐ ⓑ ⓒ ⓓ	18. ⓐ ⓑ ⓒ ⓓ	24. ⓐ ⓑ ⓒ ⓓ	30. ⓐ ⓑ ⓒ ⓓ	

Chapter 18

Sports

MCQs 1 Mark Questions

1. The Commonwealth Games started from which among the following countries?
(a) England (b) Australia
(c) Canada (d) India

2. Who among the following is the first Indian to win an individual gold medal at any Olympic Games?
(a) Abhinav Bindra
(b) Mohammed Aslam
(c) Rajyavardhan Singh Rathode
(d) Neeraj Chopra

3. Which country has won the most World Snooker Championships?
(a) Wales
(b) Scotland
(c) England
(d) Australia

4. Who won the first ICC World Cup?
(a) India (b) West Indies
(c) England (d) Australia

5. The term 'butterfly stroke' is referred to in which sport?
(a) Wrestling (b) Volleyball
(c) Tennis (d) Swimming

6. Who is regarded as the most successful Indian test captain of Indian Cricket team?
(a) Virat Kohli (b) Sunil Gavaskar
(c) MS Dhoni (d) Sachin Tendulkar

7. Ryder Cup is related with which of the following sports?
(a) Cricket (b) Badminton
(c) Golf (d) Football

8. Who is the first Indian badminton player to win an Olympic medal?
(a) Srikanth Kidambi
(b) PV Sindhu
(c) Leander Paes
(d) Saina Nehwal

9. Where is the headquarters of the International Olympic Committee located?
(a) Italy (b) France
(c) Belgium (d) Switzerland

10. Which of the following awards is not associated with the field of sports?
(a) Arjuna Award
(b) Dronacharya Award
(c) Dhyan Chand Award
(d) Norman Borlaug Award

11. The word 'Jump ball' is associated with ....

(a) softball (b) basketball
(c) netball (d) baseball

12. Which organisation oversees the Commonwealth Games?

(a) International Commonwealth Games Committee
(b) British Government
(c) Commonwealth Games Federation
(d) Association of Commonwealth Games

13. Which country became the champion of the first FIFA Women's Football World Cup held in 1991?

(a) Germany
(b) Sweden
(c) Norway
(d) United States of America

14. Michael Jordan is famous for which among the following sports?

(a) Baseball (b) Football
(c) Basketball (d) Rugby

15. Dronacharya Award is given to ....

(a) best sportsman of the year.
(b) player who won the most number of medals in a year.
(c) best team of the year.
(d) person with excellence in sports coaching.

16. Which of the following pairs is not correctly matched?

(a) Ravindra Jadeja – Cricket
(b) Manu Bhaker – Football
(c) Saina Nehwal – Badminton
(d) Somdev Devvarman – Tennis

17. Complete the given analogy.
Cricket : Pitch : : Skating : ?

(a) Arena (b) Course
(c) Court (d) Rink

18. Who was the first Indian athlete to win gold medal at Asian Games?

(a) PT Usha
(b) Lavy Pinto
(c) Kamaljeet Sandhu
(d) Tintu Luka

19. Identify the incorrectly matched pair.

(a) Wankhede Stadium, Mumbai – Cricket
(b) Shivaji Stadium, New Delhi – Hockey
(c) Dr Ambedkar Stadium, New Delhi – Cricket
(d) Dhyan Chand Stadium, Lucknow – Hockey

20. In which year, Olympics allowed females to compete in track and field events for the first time?

(a) 1920
(b) 1924
(c) 1928
(d) 1932

21. Who is considered as the Father of Modern Commonwealth Games?

(a) Melville Marks Robinson
(b) Bruce Robertson
(c) Jacques Rogge
(d) Juan Antonio Samaranch

22. In which year, the first cricket test match was played?

(a) 1876 (b) 1877
(c) 1890 (d) 1891

23. For which sport, Kidambi Srikant is famous?

(a) Tennis
(b) Cricket
(c) Hockey
(d) Badminton

24. Who became the first Indian player to win the All England Open Badminton Championship?
(a) Pullela Gopichand
(b) PV Sindhu
(c) Prakash Padukone
(d) Parupalli Kashyap

25. In which year, did India win first Olympic gold medal?
(a) 1920
(b) 1932
(c) 1928
(d) 1924

26. Who became first Indian athlete to win Olympic gold medal at track and field event?
(a) PT Usha
(b) Milkha Singh
(c) Hima Das
(d) Neeraj Chopra

27. Identify the legend whose birth anniversary is celebrated as National Sports Day.
(a) Major Dhyanchand
(b) Pullela Gopichand
(c) Kapil Dev
(d) Mohammad Ali

MCQs 2 Marks Questions

28. Consider the following statements and choose the correct option.
I. Walker Cup is associated with golf
II. There are total 5 members in a basketball team.
III. Malla-Yuddha is a traditional form of wrestling.

Codes
(a) I and II (b) II and III
(c) I and III (d) I, II and III

29. Match the following.

List I (Player)	List II (Game/Sport)
A. Roger Federar	1. Badminton
B. PV Sindhu	2. Football
C. Neymar	3. Lawn Tennis
D. Chris Gayle	4. Cricket

Codes

	A	B	C	D
(a)	3	2	1	4
(b)	4	1	2	3
(c)	3	1	2	4
(d)	4	2	1	3

30. Read the following statements and identifies which ones are true (T) and which ones are false (F).
I. The term dribbling is associated with basketball.
II. First Olympic Games were held in Greece.
III. Five rings in Olympic symbol comprises of five continents.
IV. Olympic Games are organised after every four years.

Codes

	I	II	III	IV
(a)	T	T	T	T
(b)	F	F	F	F
(c)	F	T	F	T
(d)	T	F	T	F

31. Identify the personality with the help of the information given below.

- He was a famous Indian batsman and currently serves as the coach of Indian cricket team.
- He is popularly known as Great Wall.

(a) Rahul Dravid (b) Sachin Tendulkar
(c) Sunil Gavaskar (d) Kapil Dev

32. There are two statements marked as Assertion (A) and Reason (R). Mark your answer as per the codes given below.

Assertion (A) Sumo Wrestling is the national game of Japan.

Reason (R) Sumo originated in Japan, the only country where it is practiced professionally.

Codes

(a) Both A and R are true and R is the correct explanation of A
(b) Both A and R are true, but R is not the correct explanation of A
(c) A is true, but R is false
(d) A is false, but R is true

Darken your choice with HB Pencil

1.	ⓐ ⓑ ⓒ ⓓ	7.	ⓐ ⓑ ⓒ ⓓ	13.	ⓐ ⓑ ⓒ ⓓ	19.	ⓐ ⓑ ⓒ ⓓ	25.	ⓐ ⓑ ⓒ ⓓ	31.	ⓐ ⓑ ⓒ ⓓ
2.	ⓐ ⓑ ⓒ ⓓ	8.	ⓐ ⓑ ⓒ ⓓ	14.	ⓐ ⓑ ⓒ ⓓ	20.	ⓐ ⓑ ⓒ ⓓ	26.	ⓐ ⓑ ⓒ ⓓ	32.	ⓐ ⓑ ⓒ ⓓ
3.	ⓐ ⓑ ⓒ ⓓ	9.	ⓐ ⓑ ⓒ ⓓ	15.	ⓐ ⓑ ⓒ ⓓ	21.	ⓐ ⓑ ⓒ ⓓ	27.	ⓐ ⓑ ⓒ ⓓ		
4.	ⓐ ⓑ ⓒ ⓓ	10.	ⓐ ⓑ ⓒ ⓓ	16.	ⓐ ⓑ ⓒ ⓓ	22.	ⓐ ⓑ ⓒ ⓓ	28.	ⓐ ⓑ ⓒ ⓓ		
5.	ⓐ ⓑ ⓒ ⓓ	11.	ⓐ ⓑ ⓒ ⓓ	17.	ⓐ ⓑ ⓒ ⓓ	23.	ⓐ ⓑ ⓒ ⓓ	29.	ⓐ ⓑ ⓒ ⓓ		
6.	ⓐ ⓑ ⓒ ⓓ	12.	ⓐ ⓑ ⓒ ⓓ	18.	ⓐ ⓑ ⓒ ⓓ	24.	ⓐ ⓑ ⓒ ⓓ	30.	ⓐ ⓑ ⓒ ⓓ		

Practice Set 01

Time : 60 Mins. Max. Marks : 60

General Instructions

1. This question paper contains 50 questions.
2. All questions are compulsory. There is no negative marking.
3. Q. No. 1 to 40 are of 1 mark each and Q. No. 41 to 50 are of 2 marks each.
4. Use HB pencil / Blue ball point pen to mark your choice of answer by darkening the circles on the OMR Sheet.

MCQs 1 Mark Questions

1. The system of Permanent Settlement was launched in which of the following regions in India by British?

(a) Bengal (b) Bihar
(c) Awadh (d) Madras

2. Identify the Governor-General of India who played a major role in abolition of Sati Pratha.

(a) Lord Dalhousie
(b) Lord William Bentinck
(c) Lord Cornwallis
(d) Lord Hastings

3. The Warli Movement of 1940s was popular in which of the following states?

(a) Bihar (b) Uttar Pradesh
(c) Maharashtra (d) Madras

4. Complete the given analogy.

Arya Samaj : Dayananda Saraswati : : Satyashodhak Samaj : ?

(a) Ishwar Chandra Vidyasagar
(b) Pandita Ramabai
(c) Jyotiba Phule
(d) Raja Ram Mohan Roy

5. Raja Ram Mohan Roy is associated with which among the following reforms in India?

(a) Ban on sati
(b) Encouragement of Western education
(c) Female infanticide
(d) Both (a) and (b)

6. Identify the incorrectly matched pair.

	Continents	Country
(a)	Asia	– Victnam
(b)	Europe	– Argentina
(c)	South America	– Brazil
(d)	Africa	– Morocco

7. Africa is also known as ....

(a) golden continent
(b) black continent
(c) dark continent
(d) white continent

8. The given picture is of Birsa, a leader of a popular tribal revolt. Identify the tribe to which he belonged.

(a) Santhals (b) Munda
(c) Kols (d) Bhils

9. Identify the country that does not lie in Asian continent.
(a) Singapore (b) Sri Lanka
(c) Kenya (d) Nepal

10. Who among the following was the first President of the Constituent Assembly?
(a) Dr Rajendra Prasad
(b) Dr Sachchidananda Sinha
(c) Dr BR Ambedkar
(d) Shri KM Munshi

11. Which among the following is/are the Greenhouse gases?
(a) Carbon dioxide
(b) Methane
(c) Carbon monoxide
(d) All of the above

12. Identify the national park which is the natural habitat of one horned Rhinoceros in India?
(a) Sundarbans
(b) Kaziranga National Park
(c) Periyar Wildlife Sanctuary
(d) Jim Corbett National Park

13. Identify the planet which has a largest satellite named as 'Ganymede'.
(a) Saturn (b) Earth
(c) Uranus (d) Jupiter

14. Which parameters are not important for people to be developed as a resource?
(a) Health
(b) Education
(c) Migration
(d) Skills

15. What is the meaning of the term viticulture?
(a) Cultivation of grapes
(b) Breeding of fish
(c) Cultivation of silkworms
(d) Cultivation of apples

16. Which type of farming is done in order to meet the need of the family members?
(a) Subsistence farming
(b) Mixed farming
(c) Commercial farming
(d) Inter cropping

17. Which among the following is not an activity of tertiary sector?
(a) Fishing (b) Education
(c) Health (d) Banking

18. .... is the largest coal producing state of India.
(a) Odisha (b) Bihar
(c) Jharkhand (d) Rajasthan

19. Chipko Movement was launched in which state?
(a) Himachal Pradesh
(b) Uttarakhand
(c) Jammu and Kashmir
(d) Punjab

20. Which among the following is a biodegradable waste?
(a) Cow dung (b) Plastic bag
(c) Aluminium can (d) Rubber

21. The functional unit of environment is known as ....
(a) ecosystem (b) habitat
(c) niche (d) biosphere

22. The state that does not have any official religion is known as ....
(a) secular state (b) democratic state
(c) republic (d) dictatorial state

23. Who among the following has the right to make laws on the matter of Concurrent List?
(a) Union Government
(b) State Government
(c) President of India
(d) Both (a) and (b)

24. The provision of Fundamental Duties in Indian Constitution has been borrowed from which country?
(a) USSR (b) Ireland (c) USA (d) UK

25. Identify the bill that can be introduced in Lok Sabha only.
(a) Money Bill (b) Amendment Bill
(c) Government Bill (d) Financial Bill

26. Identify the first long-range multiple-target missile in India.
(a) Prithvi (b) Agni (c) Akash (d) Brahmos

27. In which of the following situations a bill becomes a law?
(a) When the bill is signed by President
(b) When the bill is signed by Speaker
(c) When the bill is signed by Vice-President
(d) When the bill is approved by President of India

28. Who amongst the following has the power to remove a judge of a Supreme Court?
(a) Prime Minister (b) Cabinet Ministers
(c) Parliament (d) None of these

29. ……… was the first Indian to receive Nobel Prize in Literature.
(a) CV Raman (b) Mother Teresa
(c) Rabindranath Tagore (d) Sarojini Naidu

30. Identify the case that is not included under Civil Law.
(a) Property matters (b) Divorce matters
(c) Land matters (d) Murder charges

31. Who is the author of the book 'Indica'?
(a) Abu'l Fazl (b) François Bernier
(c) Megasthenes (d) Barbosa

32. The headquarters of United Nations Security Council are located in ……………
(a) New York (b) Brussels
(c) Berlin (d) Moscow

33. Hubble Space Telescope was launched by which space agency?
(a) NASA (b) European Space Agency
(c) ISRO (d) ROSCOSMOS

34. Which among the following is a pointing device?
(a) Mouse (b) Joystick
(c) Scanner (d) Both (a) and (b)

35. Which part of computer performs the function of information processing?
(a) CPU (b) Monitor
(c) Software (d) Hard Disk

36. Which among the following is India's indigenously built submarine?
(a) Arihant (b) Kalvari
(c) Sindhughosh (d) Shishumar

37. Durand Cup is associated with which sport?
(a) Cricket (b) Football
(c) Hockey (d) Tennis

38. Major Dhyan Chand's birthday is celebrated as National Sports Day in India, on which among the following dates?
(a) 29th July (b) 29th August
(c) 29th March (d) 29th April

39. In which state of India, the Silent Valley National Park is located?
(a) Karnataka (b) Kerala
(c) Tamil Nadu (d) Andhra Pradesh

40. Which of the following physical features of India forms the Northern frontiers?
(a) Aravalli Range
(b) Karakoram Range
(c) Himalayan Mountain Range
(d) Satpura Range

MCQs 2 Marks Questions

41. Consider the following statements and choose the correct option.

I. Hinayana and Mahayana are the important terms related to Buddhism.

II. According to Jaina traditions, there were 24 Tirthankaras.

III. Tripitaka are the religious text of Jainism.

Codes

(a) I and II (b) II and III

(c) I and III (d) I, II and III

42. Match the following.

List I (Tribes)	**List II** (Region)
A. Warlis	1. Maharashtra
B. Bhils	2. Rajasthan
C. Santhals	3. Odisha
D. Garo	4. Meghalaya

Codes

	A	B	C	D		A	B	C	D
(a)	1	2	3	4	(b)	2	1	4	3
(c)	3	2	4	1	(d)	4	3	1	2

43. Identify the personality with the help of the information given below.

- He founded Brahmo Samaj of India.
- His efforts towards child marriage led to enactment of Civil Marriage Act, fixing the minimum marriageable age for boys and girls.

(a) Keshab Chandra Sen

(b) Jyotiba Phule

(c) Swami Dayananda Saraswati

(d) Swami Vivekananda

44. Read the following statements and identifies which ones are true (T) and which ones are false (F).

I. Antarctica is also known as active continent.

II. Antarctica is the only continent which is fully covered with ice.

III. Antarctica is a densely populated continent.

Codes

	I	II	III		I	II	III
(a)	T	T	T	(b)	F	F	F
(c)	F	T	T	(d)	T	F	T

45. There are two statements marked as Assertion (A) and Reason (R). Mark your answer as per the codes given below.

Assertion (A) Black soils are ideal for growing cotton.

Reason (R) Black soils are volcanic in origin.

Codes

(a) Both A and R are true and R is the correct explanation of A

(b) Both A and R are true, but R is not the correct explanation of A

(c) A is true, but R is false

(d) A is false, but R is true

46. Identify the dance form that is famous in the state marked as A on the map given below.

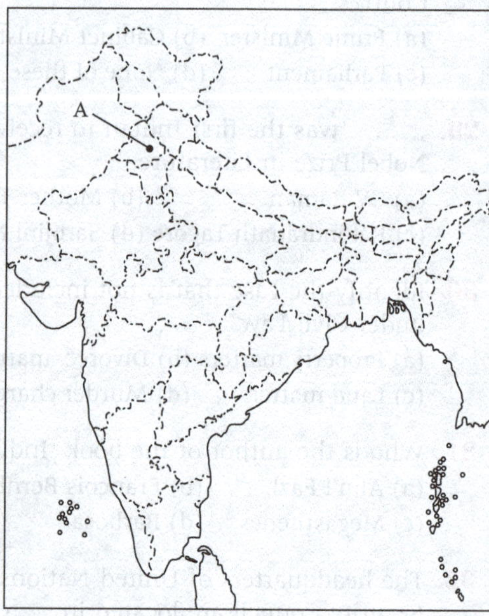

(a) Lavani (b) Gidda

(c) Garba (d) Chhau

47. There are two statements marked as Assertion (A) and Reason (R). Mark your answer as per the codes given below.

Assertion (A) Maharashtra is the leading producer of sugar in India.

Reason (R) Sugar industry is second most important agro-based industry in the world.

Codes

(a) Both A and R are true and R is the correct explanation of A

(b) Both A and R are true, but R is not the correct explanation of A

(c) A is true, but R is false

(d) A is false, but R is true

48. Consider the following statements and choose the incorrect option.

I Government defines the rules that govern the country.

II Preamble states the objectives of the government.

III Indian Independence Act, 1947 served as the background for Constitution of India.

Codes

(a) I and II (b) II and III

(c) I and III (d) I, II and III

49. Identify the personality with the help of the information given below.

- He is the author of Arthashastra.
- He was the mentor and teacher of Chandragupta Maurya and helped him to established Maurya dynasty.

(a) Ashvaghosha

(b) Chanakya

(c) Kalhana

(d) Patanjali

50. There are two statements marked as Assertion (A) and Reason (R). Mark your answer as per the codes given below.

Assertion (A) Environment includes both biotic and abiotic factors.

Reason (R) Biotic diversity is also known as ecosystem diversity.

Codes

(a) Both A and R are true and R is the correct explanation of A

(b) Both A and R are true, but R is not the correct explanation of A

(c) A is true, but R is false

(d) A is false, but R is true

Darken your choice with HB Pencil

1.	a b c d	10.	a b c d	19.	a b c d	28.	a b c d	37.	a b c d	46.	a b c d
2.	a b c d	11.	a b c d	20.	a b c d	29.	a b c d	38.	a b c d	47.	a b c d
3.	a b c d	12.	a b c d	21.	a b c d	30.	a b c d	39.	a b c d	48.	a b c d
4.	a b c d	13.	a b c d	22.	a b c d	31.	a b c d	40.	a b c d	49.	a b c d
5.	a b c d	14.	a b c d	23.	a b c d	32.	a b c d	41.	a b c d	50.	a b c d
6.	a b c d	15.	a b c d	24.	a b c d	33.	a b c d	42.	a b c d		
7.	a b c d	16.	a b c d	25.	a b c d	34.	a b c d	43.	a b c d		
8.	a b c d	17.	a b c d	26.	a b c d	35.	a b c d	44.	a b c d		
9.	a b c d	18.	a b c d	27.	a b c d	36.	a b c d	45.	a b c d		

Practice Set 02

Time : 60 Mins. Max. Marks : 60

General Instructions

1. This question paper contains 50 questions.
2. All questions are compulsory. There is no negative marking.
3. Q. No. 1 to 40 are of 1 mark each and Q. No. 41 to 50 are of 2 marks each.
4. Use HB pencil / Blue ball point pen to mark your choice of answer by darkening the circles on the OMR Sheet.

MCQs 1 Mark Questions

1. Who among the following was the last ruler of Delhi Sultanate?
(a) Qutb-ud-Din Aibak
(b) Iltutmish
(c) Alauddin Khalji
(d) Ibrahim Lodi

2. Which among the following is the world's shallowest ocean ?
(a) Pacific Ocean (b) Arctic Ocean
(c) Atlantic Ocean (d) Antarctic Ocean

3. Which of the following uprisings/rebellions is also known as Ulgulan (great commotion)?
(a) Ramosi Uprising (b) Munda Uprising
(c) Santhal Rebellion (d) Bhil Uprising

4. Who among the following was popularly known as 'Lokahitawadi'?
(a) Jyotiba Phule
(b) Ishwar Chandra Vidyasagar
(c) Gopal Hari Deshmukh
(d) Mahadev Govind Ranade

5. Identify the incorrectly matched pair.
(a) Tebhaga Movement – Lucknow
(b) Bardoli Satyagraha – Gujarat
(c) Birsa Munda Revolt – Jharkhand
(d) Eka Movement – Lucknow

6. Which continent is known as the New World?
(a) South America
(b) Asia
(c) Europe
(d) North America

7. Who is the author of famous book 'Gulamgiri'?
(a) MG Ranade
(b) Gopal Krishna Gokhale
(c) Jyotirao Phule
(d) Ishwar Chandra Vidyasagar

8. Refer to the given image and identify the ruler who completed construction of the given monument.

(a) Qutb-ud-Din Aibak
(b) Iltutmish
(c) Razia Sultan
(d) Balban

9. The world's saltiest ocean is ....
(a) Pacific Ocean (b) Arctic Ocean
(c) Atlantic Ocean (d) Antarctic Ocean

10. Identify the factor(s) that lead to the formation of soil.
(a) Temperature (b) Water
(c) Wind (d) All of these

11. Which soil is found in the Ganga-Brahmaputra delta which is the most fertile region of India?
(a) Black Soil (b) Alluvial Soil
(c) Loamy Soil (d) Laterite Soil

12. Which is the only country in the world that has the population of both tigers and lions?
(a) India (b) South Africa
(c) Bangladesh (d) Brazil

13. Complete the given analogy.
Tropical Deciduous Forests : Teak : : Montane Forests : ?
(a) Pines (b) Bamboo
(c) Sandalwood (d) Cactus

14. Which among the following regions in India has/have a high population density?
(a) Kerala (b) Northern Plains
(c) Himalayas (d) Both (a) and (b)

15. Which of the following crops are also known as coarse grains?
(a) Wheat (b) Millets
(c) Rice (d) Jute

16. Identify the input that is/are used in commercial farming methods.
(a) High yielding variety seeds
(b) Chemical fertilisers
(c) Insecticides and pesticides
(d) All of the above

17. Which among the following is not an agro-based industry?
(a) Cotton (b) Jute
(c) Petrochemicals (d) Silk

18. Which among the following is known as golden fibre of India?
(a) Jute (b) Cotton
(c) Silk (d) Wool

19. Identify the largest gold producer state of India.
(a) Maharashtra (b) Odisha
(c) Karnataka (d) Gujarat

20. Which of the following pairs is incorrectly matched?

	Biosphere Reserves	**Location**
(a)	Nilgiri Biosphere Reserve	– Tamil Nadu
(b)	Nokrek Biosphere Reserve	– Meghalaya
(c)	Similipal Biosphere Reserve	– Odisha
(d)	Dehang-Debang Biosphere Reserve	– Arunachal Pradesh

21. Kyoto Protocol is related to which among the following?
(a) Ozone depletion
(b) Climate change and reduction of greenhouse emissions
(c) Air pollution
(d) Wildlife conservation

22. Which type of forests are found in Gujarat and Rajasthan?
(a) Tropical Evergreen Forests
(b) Montane Forests
(c) Thorn Forests and Scrubs
(d) Montane Forests

23. Identify the country that does not possess a written Constitution.
(a) UK (b) USA
(c) Nepal (d) India

24. Which among the following is the foundation source of legal system in India?
(a) Judiciary (b) Parliament
(c) Constitution (d) Fundamental Rights

25. Who amongst the following moved Objective Resolution in the Constituent Assembly?
(a) Sardar Patel (b) Mahatma Gandhi
(c) Jawaharlal Nehru (d) BR Ambedkar

26. On the pattern of which among the following countries, the Parliamentary system was established in India by the Constitution of India?
(a) America (b) England
(c) Canada (d) Australia

27. Who was the first woman Governor of a state in free India?
(a) Mrs Indira Gandhi
(b) Mrs Vijaya Lakshmi Pandit
(c) Mrs Sarojini Naidu
(d) Mrs Sucheta Kripalani

28. Which is the only Union Territory that has the High Court of its own?
(a) Delhi (b) Puducherry
(c) Andaman and Nicobar (d) Ladakh

29. Judges of the High Court can hold the office till the age of ……… .
(a) 65 years (b) 62 years
(c) 50 years (d) 55 years

30. Identify the author of the famous novel series 'Harry Potter'.
(a) Charles Dickens (b) Rudyard Kipling
(c) JK Rowling (d) Ruskin Bond

31. Who is the author of the famous book 'Geetanjali'?
(a) Rabindranath Tagore
(b) Munshi Premchand
(c) R K Narayan
(d) Khushwant Singh

32. Which among the following is not a fossil fuel?
(a) Charcoal (b) Coal (c) Petrol (d) Lead

33. Identify the process by which large plants and trees buried under the Earth becomes coal.
(a) Carbonation (b) Carbueration
(c) Carbonisation (d) Carbocation

34. Which of the following computers is used at homes by individuals?
(a) Super computers
(b) Micro computers
(c) Mainframe computers
(d) Quantum computers

35. Choose the odd one out from the codes given below.
(a) LINUX (b) WINDOWS
(c) XENIX (d) SCANNER

36. The headquarters of Chief of Defence Staff are located in ……… .
(a) New Delhi (b) Visakhapatnam
(c) Mumbai (d) Chennai

37. In which of the following continents, the Andes Mountain Range is located?
(a) Australia (b) Europe
(c) South America (d) Asia

38. David Dixon Award is presented during which of the following games?
(a) Asian Games
(b) Commonwealth Games
(c) Olympic Games
(d) Paralympics

39. Feroz Shah Kotla stadium in Delhi is known for which sport?
(a) Cricket (b) Hockey
(c) Athletics (d) Football

40. Aga Khan Cup is related to which sport?
(a) Cricket (b) Football
(c) Hockey (d) Polo

MCQs 2 Marks Questions

41. Read to the following statements and choose the correct option.

I. Revolt of 1857 began in Meerut.

II. Mangal Pandey was killed during the Revolt of 1857.

III. Swadeshi Movement was launched due to Partition of Bengal.

Codes

(a) I and II (b) II and III

(c) I and III (d) I, II and III

42. Identify the personality from the description given below.

- He founded Atmiya Sabha to propogate monotheism.
- He launched a movement for abolition of Sati through his journal Sabad Kaumudi.

(a) Debendranath Tagore

(b) Raja Ram Mohan Roy

(c) Keshab Chandra Sen

(d) Atmaram Pandurang

43. Match the following.

List I (Movement)	List II (Region)
A. Indigo Revolt	1. Bengal
B. Ramosi Movement	2. Maharashtra
C. Moplah Rebellion	3. Kerala
D. Eka Movement	4. Awadh

Codes

	A	B	C	D		A	B	C	D
(a)	1	2	3	4	(b)	2	1	4	3
(c)	3	2	4	1	(d)	4	3	1	2

44. Identify the environmental factor with the help of the information given below.

- It is the phenomenon of a gradual increase in the average temperature of the Earth's atmosphere and its water bodies.
- The leading cause for this environmental issue is the increased volumes of greenhouse gases in the atmosphere.

(a) Solid waste pollution

(b) Global warming

(c) Deforestation

(d) Climate change

45. Refer to the marking in the given map and identify the industry that was first established in the below marked region.

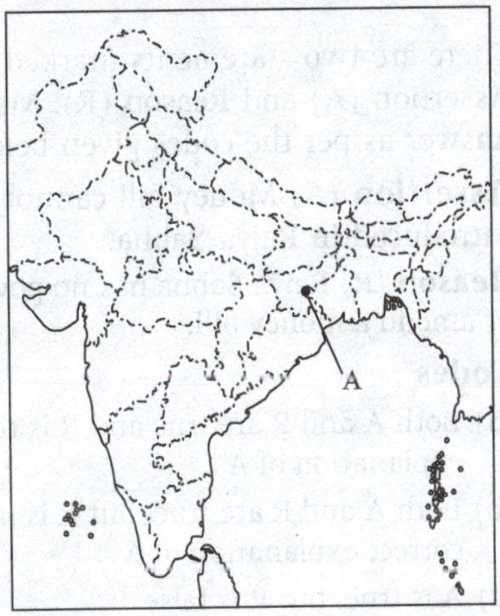

(a) TISCO

(b) BHEL

(c) Indian Oil Corporation

(d) Reliance Industries

46. There are two statements marked as Assertion (A) and Reason (R). Mark your answer as per the codes given below.

Assertion (A) Intensive subsistence farming is practiced in high population areas.

Reason (R) Intensive subsistence farming is a labour intensive farming.

Codes

(a) Both A and R are true and R is the correct explanation of A

(b) Both A and R are true, but R is not the correct explanation of A

(c) A is true, but R is false

(d) A is false, but R is true

47. Read the following statements and choose the correct option.

I. The Blue Revolution is related to fish production.

II. Silver Fibre Revolution is related to cotton production.

III. Green Revolution is related to food grains production in India.

Codes

(a) Only I (b) I and II

(c) Only III (d) I, II and III

48. There are two statements marked as Assertion (A) and Reason (R). Mark your answer as per the codes given below.

Assertion (A) Money bill cannot be introduced in Rajya Sabha.

Reason (R) Rajya Sabha has no power to reject or amend a money bill.

Codes

(a) Both A and R are true and R is the correct explanation of A

(b) Both A and R are true, but R is not the correct explanation of A

(c) A is true, but R is false

(b) A is false, but R is true

49. Read the following statements and choose the correct option.

I. The oath to a High Court Judge is administered by the Governor of the concerned state.

II. Judge of High Court is appointed by Chief Justice of Supreme Court.

III. Supreme Court is the highest authority of interpretation of Constitution of India.

Codes

(a) I and II

(b) II and III

(c) I and III

(d) I, II and III

50. There are two statements marked as Assertion (A) and Reason (R). Mark your answer as per the codes given below.

I. The Constitution of a country is a set of written rules that are accepted by all the people living in a country.

II. The Indian Constitution came into force with effect from 26th January, 1950.

III. Article 345 of the Indian Constitution deals with the official language or language of a state.

Codes

	I	II	III
(a)	T	T	T
(b)	T	F	T
(c)	F	T	F
(d)	F	F	F

Darken your choice with HB Pencil

1.	ⓐ ⓑ ⓒ ⓓ	10.	ⓐ ⓑ ⓒ ⓓ	19.	ⓐ ⓑ ⓒ ⓓ	28.	ⓐ ⓑ ⓒ ⓓ	37.	ⓐ ⓑ ⓒ ⓓ	46.	ⓐ ⓑ ⓒ ⓓ
2.	ⓐ ⓑ ⓒ ⓓ	11.	ⓐ ⓑ ⓒ ⓓ	20.	ⓐ ⓑ ⓒ ⓓ	29.	ⓐ ⓑ ⓒ ⓓ	38.	ⓐ ⓑ ⓒ ⓓ	47.	ⓐ ⓑ ⓒ ⓓ
3.	ⓐ ⓑ ⓒ ⓓ	12.	ⓐ ⓑ ⓒ ⓓ	21.	ⓐ ⓑ ⓒ ⓓ	30.	ⓐ ⓑ ⓒ ⓓ	39.	ⓐ ⓑ ⓒ ⓓ	48.	ⓐ ⓑ ⓒ ⓓ
4.	ⓐ ⓑ ⓒ ⓓ	13.	ⓐ ⓑ ⓒ ⓓ	22.	ⓐ ⓑ ⓒ ⓓ	31.	ⓐ ⓑ ⓒ ⓓ	40.	ⓐ ⓑ ⓒ ⓓ	49.	ⓐ ⓑ ⓒ ⓓ
5.	ⓐ ⓑ ⓒ ⓓ	14.	ⓐ ⓑ ⓒ ⓓ	23.	ⓐ ⓑ ⓒ ⓓ	32.	ⓐ ⓑ ⓒ ⓓ	41.	ⓐ ⓑ ⓒ ⓓ	50.	ⓐ ⓑ ⓒ ⓓ
6.	ⓐ ⓑ ⓒ ⓓ	15.	ⓐ ⓑ ⓒ ⓓ	24.	ⓐ ⓑ ⓒ ⓓ	33.	ⓐ ⓑ ⓒ ⓓ	42.	ⓐ ⓑ ⓒ ⓓ		
7.	ⓐ ⓑ ⓒ ⓓ	16.	ⓐ ⓑ ⓒ ⓓ	25.	ⓐ ⓑ ⓒ ⓓ	34.	ⓐ ⓑ ⓒ ⓓ	43.	ⓐ ⓑ ⓒ ⓓ		
8.	ⓐ ⓑ ⓒ ⓓ	17.	ⓐ ⓑ ⓒ ⓓ	26.	ⓐ ⓑ ⓒ ⓓ	35.	ⓐ ⓑ ⓒ ⓓ	44.	ⓐ ⓑ ⓒ ⓓ		
9.	ⓐ ⓑ ⓒ ⓓ	18.	ⓐ ⓑ ⓒ ⓓ	27.	ⓐ ⓑ ⓒ ⓓ	36.	ⓐ ⓑ ⓒ ⓓ	45.	ⓐ ⓑ ⓒ ⓓ		

Answer Sheet

Chapter 01

1. (b)	**2.** (c)	**3.** (d)	**4.** (b)	**5.** (c)	**6.** (a)	**7.** (a)	**8.** (a)	**9.** (b)	**10.** (b)
11. (a)	**12.** (a)	**13.** (b)	**14.** (b)	**15.** (a)	**16.** (c)	**17.** (a)	**18.** (d)	**19.** (a)	**20.** (c)
21. (a)	**22.** (a)	**23.** (b)	**24.** (b)	**25.** (d)	**26.** (b)	**27.** (a)	**28.** (d)	**29.** (c)	**30.** (c)
31. (a)	**32.** (b)	**33.** (a)	**34.** (a)	**35.** (a)	**36.** (c)	**37.** (c)	**38.** (a)	**39.** (a)	**40.** (c)
41. (b)	**42.** (b)	**43.** (a)							

Chapter 02

1. (a)	**2.** (a)	**3.** (a)	**4.** (d)	**5.** (b)	**6.** (d)	**7.** (b)	**8.** (a)	**9.** (b)	**10.** (d)
11. (b)	**12.** (c)	**13.** (a)	**14.** (b)	**15.** (b)	**16.** (a)	**17.** (c)	**18.** (c)	**19.** (c)	**20.** (a)
21. (d)	**22.** (d)	**23.** (b)							

Chapter 03

1. (a)	**2.** (b)	**3.** (a)	**4.** (a)	**5.** (a)	**6.** (b)	**7.** (d)	**8.** (a)	**9.** (a)	**10.** (d)
11. (b)	**12.** (a)	**13.** (c)	**14.** (a)	**15.** (d)	**16.** (c)	**17.** (a)	**18.** (d)	**19.** (c)	**20.** (a)
21. (a)	**22.** (a)	**23.** (c)	**24.** (a)	**25.** (d)	**26.** (c)	**27.** (a)			

Chapter 04

1. (b)	**2.** (a)	**3.** (b)	**4.** (a)	**5.** (b)	**6.** (c)	**7.** (d)	**8.** (c)	**9.** (b)	**10.** (b)
11. (a)	**12.** (c)	**13.** (b)	**14.** (d)	**15.** (a)	**16.** (b)	**17.** (c)	**18.** (a)	**19.** (d)	**20.** (a)
21. (c)	**22.** (c)	**23.** (a)	**24.** (a)	**25.** (c)	**26.** (a)	**27.** (c)	**28.** (a)	**29.** (b)	**30.** (a)

Chapter 05

1. (a)	**2.** (d)	**3.** (b)	**4.** (d)	**5.** (d)	**6.** (a)	**7.** (c)	**8.** (c)	**9.** (b)	**10.** (a)
11. (b)	**12.** (d)	**13.** (b)	**14.** (b)	**15.** (a)	**16.** (d)	**17.** (d)	**18.** (c)	**19.** (b)	**20.** (d)
21. (a)	**22.** (a)	**23.** (b)							

Chapter 06

1. (d)	**2.** (b)	**3.** (b)	**4.** (a)	**5.** (a)	**6.** (a)	**7.** (d)	**8.** (c)	**9.** (b)	**10.** (c)
11. (b)	**12.** (a)	**13.** (d)	**14.** (a)	**15.** (a)	**16.** (d)	**17.** (a)	**18.** (a)	**19.** (b)	**20.** (b)
21. (c)	**22.** (b)	**23.** (a)	**24.** (a)	**25.** (a)	**26.** (c)				

Chapter 07

1. (b)	**2.** (a)	**3.** (c)	**4.** (b)	**5.** (b)	**6.** (c)	**7.** (c)	**8.** (d)	**9.** (b)	**10.** (b)
11. (d)	**12.** (b)	**13.** (a)	**14.** (d)	**15.** (a)	**16.** (a)	**17.** (a)	**18.** (d)	**19.** (d)	**20.** (c)
21. (a)	**22.** (a)	**23.** (a)							

Chapter 08

1. (d)	**2.** (a)	**3.** (a)	**4.** (b)	**5.** (b)	**6.** (a)	**7.** (d)	**8.** (d)	**9.** (a)	**10.** (b)
11. (b)	**12.** (b)	**13.** (a)	**14.** (b)	**15.** (d)	**16.** (a)	**17.** (a)	**18.** (a)	**19.** (c)	**20.** (b)
21. (d)	**22.** (b)	**23.** (a)	**24.** (a)	**25.** (a)	**26.** (a)	**27.** (d)	**28.** (c)	**29.** (b)	**30.** (b)
31. (b)	**32.** (c)								

Chapter 09

1. (b)	**2.** (a)	**3.** (a)	**4.** (c)	**5.** (c)	**6.** (c)	**7.** (d)	**8.** (b)	**9.** (c)	**10.** (c)
11. (a)	**12.** (a)	**13.** (a)	**14.** (c)	**15.** (c)	**16.** (a)	**17.** (d)	**18.** (b)	**19.** (d)	**20.** (b)
21. (b)	**22.** (a)	**23.** (a)	**24.** (c)	**25.** (a)	**26.** (d)	**27.** (b)	**28.** (a)	**29.** (a)	

Chapter 10

1. (b)	**2.** (a)	**3.** (a)	**4.** (d)	**5.** (b)	**6.** (a)	**7.** (b)	**8.** (c)	**9.** (c)	**10.** (a)
11. (b)	**12.** (a)	**13.** (b)	**14.** (c)	**15.** (b)	**16.** (a)	**17.** (b)	**18.** (c)	**19.** (d)	**20.** (d)
21. (d)	**22.** (d)	**23.** (d)	**24.** (a)	**25.** (c)	**26.** (a)	**27.** (b)	**28.** (c)		

Chapter 11

1. (c)	**2.** (c)	**3.** (a)	**4.** (b)	**5.** (a)	**6.** (c)	**7.** (a)	**8.** (b)	**9.** (a)	**10.** (d)
11. (a)	**12.** (a)	**13.** (a)	**14.** (b)	**15.** (a)	**16.** (b)	**17.** (c)	**18.** (c)	**19.** (a)	**20.** (a)
21. (b)	**22.** (c)	**23.** (b)	**24.** (c)	**25.** (b)	**26.** (d)	**27.** (b)	**28.** (a)		

Chapter 12

1. (c)	**2.** (b)	**3.** (a)	**4.** (b)	**5.** (b)	**6.** (b)	**7.** (d)	**8.** (a)	**9.** (c)	**10.** (a)
11. (c)	**12.** (a)	**13.** (b)	**14.** (a)	**15.** (d)	**16.** (d)	**17.** (b)	**18.** (c)	**19.** (c)	**20.** (c)
21. (b)	**22.** (d)	**23.** (c)	**24.** (a)	**25.** (c)	**26.** (d)	**27.** (d)	**28.** (b)	**29.** (a)	**30.** (d)
31. (d)	**32.** (b)								

Chapter 13

1. (a)	**2.** (d)	**3.** (c)	**4.** (a)	**5.** (c)	**6.** (a)	**7.** (d)	**8.** (a)	**9.** (a)	**10.** (c)
11. (b)	**12.** (c)	**13.** (d)	**14.** (b)	**15.** (a)	**16.** (a)	**17.** (d)	**18.** (d)	**19.** (a)	**20.** (c)
21. (c)	**22.** (d)	**23.** (d)	**24.** (b)	**25.** (a)	**26.** (d)	**27.** (d)			

Chapter 14

1. (c)	**2.** (c)	**3.** (c)	**4.** (b)	**5.** (d)	**6.** (c)	**7.** (a)	**8.** (a)	**9.** (c)	**10.** (a)
11. (d)	**12.** (b)	**13.** (c)	**14.** (b)	**15.** (c)	**16.** (a)	**17.** (b)	**18.** (d)	**19.** (d)	**20.** (a)
21. (a)	**22.** (c)	**23.** (c)	**24.** (d)	**25.** (c)	**26.** (b)	**27.** (a)	**28.** (b)	**29.** (a)	**30.** (c)
31. (b)	**32.** (b)	**33.** (a)	**34.** (d)	**35.** (c)	**36.** (a)				

Chapter 15

1. (a)	**2.** (a)	**3.** (a)	**4.** (b)	**5.** (d)	**6.** (a)	**7.** (c)	**8.** (c)	**9.** (b)	**10.** (b)
11. (d)	**12.** (d)	**13.** (c)	**14.** (c)	**15.** (b)	**16.** (d)	**17.** (c)	**18.** (a)	**19.** (c)	**20.** (b)
21. (b)	**22.** (d)	**23.** (a)	**24.** (a)	**25.** (c)	**26.** (a)	**27.** (c)	**28.** (c)	**29.** (d)	**30.** (a)
31. (b)	**32.** (b)	**33.** (d)							

Chapter 16

1. (b)	**2.** (d)	**3.** (c)	**4.** (a)	**5.** (b)	**6.** (c)	**7.** (d)	**8.** (c)	**9.** (b)	**10.** (c)
11. (b)	**12.** (c)	**13.** (b)	**14.** (c)	**15.** (a)	**16.** (a)	**17.** (b)	**18.** (d)	**19.** (d)	**20.** (d)
21. (b)	**22.** (a)	**23.** (c)	**24.** (a)	**25.** (b)	**26.** (d)	**27.** (b)	**28.** (b)	**29.** (c)	**30.** (a)

Chapter 17

1. (d)	**2.** (c)	**3.** (b)	**4.** (a)	**5.** (b)	**6.** (c)	**7.** (b)	**8.** (a)	**9.** (c)	**10.** (c)
11. (d)	**12.** (d)	**13.** (a)	**14.** (b)	**15.** (b)	**16.** (a)	**17.** (d)	**18.** (c)	**19.** (d)	**20.** (b)
21. (d)	**22.** (a)	**23.** (b)	**24.** (c)	**25.** (a)	**26.** (c)	**27.** (c)	**28.** (d)	**29.** (b)	**30.** (b)
31. (a)									

Chapter 18

1. (c)	**2.** (a)	**3.** (c)	**4.** (b)	**5.** (d)	**6.** (c)	**7.** (c)	**8.** (d)	**9.** (d)	**10.** (d)
11. (b)	**12.** (c)	**13.** (d)	**14.** (c)	**15.** (d)	**16.** (b)	**17.** (d)	**18.** (c)	**19.** (c)	**20.** (c)
21. (a)	**22.** (b)	**23.** (d)	**24.** (c)	**25.** (c)	**26.** (d)	**27.** (a)	**28.** (d)	**29.** (c)	**30.** (a)
31. (a)	**32.** (b)								

Practice Set 01

1. (a)	**2.** (b)	**3.** (c)	**4.** (c)	**5.** (d)	**6.** (b)	**7.** (c)	**8.** (b)	**9.** (c)	**10.** (b)
11. (d)	**12.** (b)	**13.** (d)	**14.** (c)	**15.** (a)	**16.** (a)	**17.** (a)	**18.** (c)	**19.** (b)	**20.** (a)
21. (a)	**22.** (a)	**23.** (d)	**24.** (a)	**25.** (a)	**26.** (c)	**27.** (a)	**28.** (d)	**29.** (c)	**30.** (d)
31. (c)	**32.** (a)	**33.** (a)	**34.** (d)	**35.** (a)	**36.** (a)	**37.** (b)	**38.** (b)	**39.** (b)	**40.** (c)
41. (a)	**42.** (a)	**43.** (a)	**44.** (a)	**45.** (b)	**46.** (b)	**47.** (b)	**48.** (d)	**49.** (b)	**50.** (b)

Practice Set 02

1. (d)	**2.** (b)	**3.** (b)	**4.** (c)	**5.** (a)	**6.** (d)	**7.** (c)	**8.** (b)	**9.** (c)	**10.** (d)
11. (b)	**12.** (a)	**13.** (a)	**14.** (d)	**15.** (b)	**16.** (d)	**17.** (c)	**18.** (a)	**19.** (c)	**20.** (a)
21. (b)	**22.** (c)	**23.** (a)	**24.** (c)	**25.** (c)	**26.** (b)	**27.** (c)	**28.** (a)	**29.** (b)	**30.** (c)
31. (a)	**32.** (d)	**33.** (c)	**34.** (b)	**35.** (d)	**36.** (a)	**37.** (c)	**38.** (b)	**39.** (a)	**40.** (c)
41. (d)	**42.** (b)	**43.** (a)	**44.** (b)	**45.** (a)	**46.** (b)	**47.** (d)	**48.** (b)	**49.** (d)	**50.** (a)